Unlocking your Child's Genius

How to discover and encourage your child's natural talents

Andrew Fuller

1 3 5 7 9 10 8 6 4 2

Vermilion, an imprint of Ebury Publishing,
20 Vauxhall Bridge Road,
London SW1V 2SA

Vermilion is part of the Penguin Random House group of companies
whose addresses can be found at global.penguinrandomhouse.com

Penguin
Random House
UK

First published in the United Kingdom by Vermilion in 2016
First published in Australia and New Zealand by Finch Publishing in 2015

www.eburypublishing.co.uk

A CIP catalogue record for this book is available from the British Library

ISBN 9781785040733

Printed and bound in Great Britain by Clays Ltd, St Ives PLC

Penguin Random House is committed to a sustainable future for our
business, our readers and our planet. This book is made from Forest
Stewardship Council® certified paper.

Contents

If you want your children to be brilliant, read them fairy stories. If you want them to be even more brilliant, read them more fairy stories.

Albert Einstein

For all the parents, grandparents, aunts and uncles who don't realise they are the most important teachers of all.

The most important message you can give your child

You are a living legend. You have a brain that is capable of sheer genius. Think of the smartest person you can and know that you have that potential, too. You are just as capable, just as creative and just as clever.

But you can't rely on your brains alone. You are going to have to try, and to keep trying. You won't pass every test with flying colours, or win every competition or be picked for every team. You will need to work and practise and improve.

You do not need to be successful at everything you do. In fact, the times you make mistakes, get things wrong or don't get the results you want can be used to make you even smarter.

There will be times when you will feel like giving up on the things that you want. These times will test you. But you need to keep going. Find the strength within you. It is there; look for it.

There will be things that you will think are too hard for you to do. You will be tempted to not do these things thinking it is better not to try than to fail. Often this will be your anxious brain trying to get you out of something.

If it is something you really want or is very important to you, don't let your brain talk you out of doing it. Take the risk and even if you don't achieve what you want the first or second time you try, you will learn more about how to achieve it next time.

Learning is some of the best fun there is. Try to find ways to make learning interesting, even the boring bits. If you surround yourself with good ideas, great books, art, films and terrific conversations, your brain will amaze you.

Most times it is easy to get interested in learning something but sometimes the only way is to challenge yourself by seeing how much you can remember or understand.

Most of all, know that I love you the same whether you win or lose. I want you to have an amazing life because I know you are capable of it.

I love you and believe in you.

Introduction

A child is a fire to be lit, not a vase to be filled.

François Rabelais

In the great expanse of desert that Aboriginal Australians inhabit, fire plays a major role. As the wet season approaches, dark billowing clouds roll in and the night air rumbles with thunder and crackles with lightning that sparks from one horizon to the other. On these lush humid evenings, Lightning Man dances.

According to Bilawara, an Elder of the Larrakia people, the creation and maintenance of fire has always been important for her people. Making fire takes patience and effort. Sometimes it was obtained from lightning strikes that were seen as a gift from the Lightning Brothers. This gift must not be wasted, so the glowing fire sticks were carried from camp to camp, transferring the spark from site to site.

These rituals can also be likened to unlocking your child's genius. Parents can nourish and feed their child's curiosity and abilities by exploring the world with them and transferring these sparks of genius when possible. At first the task of fuelling genius is time-consuming, but easy. Following a child's interests, watching as they set ideas alight, and encouraging them to take hold and gain strength fills the heart with wonder.

All too often, however, in middle childhood the initial fires of genius that burned so brightly falter and there is a risk that they may become snuffed out. If this happens children dim down, fear trying new things and worry about making mistakes. Sadly, they are left with a stunted version of their abilities – and themselves.

At this time the power of parents to ignite the blaze of brilliance becomes truly inspiring. Fortunately you have at your fingertips the best laboratory for unlocking your child's genius – it's called the world. By exploring, creating and playing in it, you can expand your child's mind. By taking time with them to delight and wonder and be curious, you ignite sparks that will flicker and flourish throughout their lives. What a gift to give.

This book is designed to help you to raise your children to discover their full potential. All children have far greater capacity and inner genius than either they or we realise. This book is about ways to unlocking that potential. It is **NOT** about rushing them, fast-tracking them, hothousing them or having them leap years ahead at school. It is about raising them intentionally to let their natural genius flourish. It's a book about parenting children so they can blossom and develop into their own form of creative, imaginative genius. As you will see in the chapters that follow, this is much more about play, fun and exploration than it is about work. Hard work has its place of course, but it is much more likely to be successful when we convert parts of it into play.

It wasn't so many years ago that we thought brains stopped developing at around the age of eight. Modern neuroscience has made that idea as unbelievable as the idea that the earth is flat. The idea that intelligence was something you got at birth and couldn't do much about has also been shaken by the same area of science.

To add to this turmoil, our modern understandings of the term 'genius' are looking wobbly. Before the Middle Ages, genius was seen as an innate spark or characteristic of inquisitiveness within all people. Since that time the term has been increasingly used to describe a small group of elite people who possess skills at a lofty level while the rest of us non-geniuses sit around twiddling our thumbs and waiting for the bright guys and girls to come up with the answers.

You don't have to spend too long hanging out with so-called geniuses to realise they also possess areas of great ignorance and stupidity. Similarly, you don't have to spend too long working with children who are labelled not-so-clever to learn that most, if not all, have areas of incredible creativity and skill.

Every child can develop the skills and knowledge base to bring to the fore every iota of genius available to them. In the following chapters I cover the skills parents can help to develop in children that will apply in whatever direction the child's interests and passions take them.

Self-knowledge, concentration, decision-making, imagination, motivation, determination, memory and creativity are the foundation skills everyone needs if they are to unlock their genius.

Your child's genius will only be unlocked when you take the time to plan, enrich, explore and help them discover their spark. In a world that requires children to study more and play less, we need to help them play more, reflect, consider and analyse more – and, most of all, dream bigger dreams.

To consider what parents can do to ignite this spark we need to add to our analogy of the fire guardians of Aboriginal Australia with the good old half-glass of water concept.

As we know, your point of view is critically important. What can you see in the image on the next page? While the optimists are looking at the glass as half full and the pessimists are seeing the glass as half empty, the opportunists are drinking the water.

After many years of working with young people, I know that you can't do much with the top half of the glass. What you *can do* is to discover what is in your child's glass and help him or her to make more of it. Whether you want to think of it as the charge in their battery, the fire in their belly, the passion in their heart or the petrol in their tank, the point is that you need to take that strength and build on it.

If you adopt the ideas in this book you will be out of step with what most parents do. We live in a world where television screens get larger but children get fatter, more anxious and timid and less happy. Schools rank children on marks in literacy, numeracy

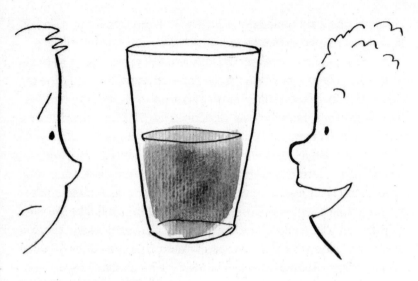

Is your glass half full or half empty?

and science rather than key issues that predict genius – effort, determination, imagination and the willingness to make mistakes and keep going. The effectiveness of schools is not even based on children's ability to impart the skills that predict academic success: positive relationships, the ability to identify similarities and differences, note-making, and giving and utilising feedback.

This book is not designed to be read in a rush or all in one go. Please take *Unlocking Your Child's Genius* on as a slow read to be digested over time. There are things that you can act on in this book that will create an immediate impact on your child's genius while others are longer-term projects that take time to weave their magic.

For example, one of the most powerful ways you can help your child develop is to give them the opportunity to have a range of experiences. Have a look through the experiences listed at the end of Chapter 2 and make a list of activities you plan to do with your child over the next few months. Other high impact things that you can do immediately are outlined in Chapter 14 (Powering up the genius brain) and Chapter 15 (Setting up family routines and rituals).

At the end of most chapters I've included tables that give you some ideas for experiences, games and activities that will engage and inspire children, and help to unlock their inner genius. Go through the lists of these ideas, marking those that you have already done with your child and circling those that you plan to do in the coming months.

The longer-term projects take more time but they don't need to be daunting. Building creativity, ingenuity and character are lifelong projects. If you are able to take on a process of sustained parenting to bring out a child's genius, read a chapter at a time and think about how you can create changes and opportunities for you and your child. Remember the lesson of the hare and the tortoise – slow and steady wins the race.

Best wishes, play and have fun!

Andrew Fuller

Please note that while I use the term parent throughout this book, I am referring to any adult – parent, grandparent, aunt, uncle or carer – who is raising or caring for a child.

CHAPTER 1

Nurturing genius – your role

> *A schoolboy was asked by his teacher why he was late to*
> *school. The boy said, 'It was so wet and slippery that every*
> *time I took one step forward I slid two steps back.' The*
> *teacher haughtily asked, 'So how come you are at school?'*
> *The boy replied, 'I turned around and headed for home*
> *and ended up here!'*

Our children are geniuses. You may not realise it. They almost certainly don't. But our children are part of the brightest generation of humans ever. They are humanity's latest upgrade.

Our children are 40 per cent brighter than the average young person was in 1950. On average, scores on intelligence (IQ) measures have increased by 3 points every decade in the last century. This trend continues and may even be accelerating.

Add to this the enormous amount of technology we use now to leverage and increase our mental powers – laptops, smartphones, the internet – and the shift really is an exponential explosion of intelligence. It is estimated that we process five times more information every day than people did in 1986.

This gain in intelligence has been achieved without any targeted intervention. Imagine what gains we could see if we helped to nourish our children's cleverness rather than passively waiting for their abilities to unfurl like leaves in the springtime.

Geniuses in the 21st century resemble the multi-skilled artists of the Renaissance era more than any other time in history. Today's geniuses are thought-weavers. They are able to access knowledge from multiple sources, integrate it in ingenious ways and apply it in innovative ways in multiple settings.

You are your child's most important teacher

Don't rely solely on schools to unlock your children's genius: you are their first and most important teacher.

Teachers and schools do their best for children but their impact is extended over many students at a time. Schools are constrained by guidelines and budgets. Some educational bureaucracies can be slow to adopt new research on how people learn and new methods for utilising that knowledge in classrooms. Children can soar when parents add to the efforts of teachers in building skills, interests, passions and concentration.

Children spend only between 10 and 15 per cent of their time at school. They spend more time asleep (33 per cent) than they do at school. The rest of their time (52 per cent) is at home, awake, mucking around, playing and learning about life. It's what they do with that time that makes the most significant impact on their development.

The people who can most powerfully unlock your genius are the people who play with them, spend the most time with them and love them the most – you.

Most of your child's future learning also won't occur in school. It is estimated that most of the jobs that will exist in the year 2030 do not exist now. Knowledge doubles every three years. It is estimated that 50 years ago a secondary school graduate left school knowing about 75 per cent of the information they would use in their working lives. In contrast today's secondary school graduate will leave knowing about 2 per cent!

To prepare our children for success now and in the future, we need to help them to become people who are able and interested in learning.

Our children will need to think creatively to devise solutions to problems we haven't even considered let alone encountered. This means that we need to think about how we can raise citizens who are able to reflect deeply on important issues, to deal with the demands of the changing world.

It seems highly likely that geniuses in the 21st century will need to be able to take wisdom, rather than information, from multiple sources, combine and rearrange it in new ways and then apply those thoughts and solutions to new and unforeseen challenges.

The lights were on, now no-one's home

Watch little kids learn. They have energy to burn and a rage to learn. They investigate everything, turn houses upside down, dream up wild adventures, see connections between things that are incredible and exhaust their parents.

Attitudes towards inquisitiveness are formed before school begins. For example, four-year-olds ask a 'why' question on average every two minutes in their homes but at preschool, the same children ask far fewer questions – about two or three every hour.

Let's now time travel forwards to secondary school. Many teenagers are slumped over their desks, bored, listless and not prepared to try anything in case they get something wrong and are ridiculed by their friends. Even worse, some are hiding away their genius because they don't want to be shunned by their friends for being too smart.

Say we ask two sets of school students the following question: We have a flock of seventeen sheep and three wolves come along, how old is the shepherd? Most Year 1 pupils say, 'Who knows?'

Depressingly high numbers of secondary school students answer, 'Twenty'. Somehow, they have stopped thinking.

This slump in motivation to explore new ideas has its origins around the middle of primary school. You can even see signs of it in preschool when girls regularly say mathematics is more important for boys than girls!

What has happened to these young minds? Natural curiosity has been dimmed and imagination has been thwarted. Our children's creativity has been killed by our desire to rank people. Throughout history humans seem to have been determined to rank people and place them into hierarchies. Every human society seems to want to play 'Who is better than someone else'. This might have been useful when selecting the best runner, hunter or cook in a tribal society, but its cost to the modern world is high.

Children become aware of this system of ranking very early on. It is done to them and they do it to one another. They become even more acutely tuned into what is important to the adults around them.

This is why it is easy to turn an eager learner into a disinterested one very quickly. Some children decide it is preferable to be average and to fit in with their friends. Some become so accustomed to being rewarded for learning that they lose the enjoyment of learning. Others decide that school is not a place where they can succeed.

The cost of rankings and comparisons is that children limit their intelligence, become less curious, ask fewer questions, dim down and have less contact with their inner genius. They may also become more cautious and worried.

The growing capability of children to think logically and to be aware of consequences all too often is converted into anxiety rather than imagination.

If the thought of being the most important teacher in your child's life is daunting, don't be worried. All it requires is for you to be clear in your intentions as a parent in a way that most people rarely are. Planning to gradually expose your child to experiences, stories, pictures, ideas and skills that will help him or her to discover their inner genius doesn't mean it is hard work, but it does mean you need to have a plan.

This book will give you the plan. You don't need to know all of the answers but you do need to be brave enough to unlock your child's natural talents in your own dynamic way.

Throwing away some crazy ideas

As you are your child's most important teacher, it's important to give your own head a spring clean. It is time to chuck out some of the ideas that you might have picked up about what makes a genius.

Crazy idea #1: Intelligence is something you can't change

At school, children learn that there is only one answer, the teacher knows the correct answer and it is in the back of the book. Author and speaker Sir Ken Robinson says most children are geniuses but schools and society work actively to shut them down. Studies of divergent thinking (the type of creative thinking that involves considering how many uses you could have for a feather duster) demonstrate that young children are capable of dreaming up new possibilities at genius level but that this ability steadily declines over the school years. We move from a world of many answers to a world of one correct answer. In the process we close minds down. The question is, what can we do to open them up again?

A lot of people think they are born with a set amount of intelligence and that they have to 'like it or lump it'. Not true. Even our children can think like this. Intelligence is not fixed and alters over your life span. For example, we know that children are getting cleverer. Average IQ rates go up every ten years.

We know a lot more now than we did ten years ago about how brains learn. Our knowledge of the processes of neuroplasticity, which the brain uses to generate itself, and myelination, which allows us to think faster and more efficiently, has transformed our understanding of brain development. Experiences drive these processes and if we can give children access to these experiences we can help them to become much, much smarter.

This is why schools should not resemble the schools many of us attended years ago. It is also why parents as well as teachers are the 'neuro-architects' of their children's brains.

This doesn't mean rushing your children to learn before their time and it certainly doesn't mean pressuring them to be the fastest reader, the youngest writer or the slickest number cruncher. Rather, it's giving them opportunities to discover that learning can be fun.

It is a lot more fulfilling as a parent to stimulate and build curiosity than to ram information into a closed mind. It's important to expand children's minds, but not accelerate them.

Do our children already think they can't get any smarter?

If your child shows any of the following signs they may not understand that they can get much smarter:

- are reluctant to try new things
- give up as soon as they make a mistake
- feel the only way to build themselves up is to make someone else feel small
- seem anxious and fearful of making mistakes.

Do these apply to anyone you know? Maybe they also apply to you. It would hardly be surprising since society seems to have been lured into a conspiracy to make people forget how clever they really are.

Crazy idea #2: Genius and creativity are things only a small group of people have

Most people have been trained to believe that genius and creativity are things other people possess. Many people believe that creative people are born with a special gift and incorrectly conclude that they are just not one of those lucky people.

Traditionally genius was seen as a guiding spirit that everyone possessed. It was only in the 14th century that people began to see genius as a rare attribute possessed by a lucky few. There are two problems with our current way of viewing genius. The first problem is it converts genius into an exclusive club that most of us can never dream of entering. The second is that it is just not true.

Many people who have made exceptional contributions did not possess Da Vinci-like all-round capabilities or do especially well at school. Many had only a few illustrious moments in their careers. Some people who have been labelled as geniuses received accolades during their lifetime (such as Pablo Picasso, Stephen Hawking, Rudolph Nureyev and Margot Fonteyn, Bill Gates and Steve Jobs) but many others were either dismissed or forgotten: Vincent Van Gogh, Mark Lidwill (the first inventor of the pacemaker), John O'Sullivan (the inventor of wi-fi), as well as the scientists at Australia's CSIRO who developed the ultrasound.

Most great things have very simple beginnings. An idea or concept is refined and built upon over time. Beethoven's symphonies started out as a couple of notes on a piano. It took Shakespeare quite some time before he worked out exactly what was wrong in the state of Denmark.

It is far healthier to think, 'Well, if most wonderful things had very simple beginnings, I am a fairly simple person therefore I am capable of creating great things.'

Crazy idea #3: Mistakes are bad

No-one plays 'Ode to Joy' perfectly on his or her first try. People fumble around making mistakes that they refine as they go.

In fact, you can't be a genius if you can't get things wrong. You have to get things wrong in order to get them right. Creativity and discovery are about getting something wrong, then shaping it and honing it until it becomes something wonderful.

Crazy idea #4: Geniuses had parents who were geniuses

You don't have to be especially clever to raise a genius. Most of our recognised geniuses grew up in fairly humble homes in the presence of parents who weren't renowned for anything in particular. Generally, their parents were interested in learning and improving and growing – and encouraged their children to do the same.

- Benjamin Franklin came from a family of candle makers.
- Abraham Lincoln was born in a one-bedroom cabin to uneducated parents.
- Walt Disney's father was often penniless and destitute.
- Oprah Winfrey was born into abject poverty.

Whether you regard these people as geniuses or not, it is clear that you don't have to come from a highly intellectual background in order to succeed. So if you don't always feel like you are the sharpest tool in the shed, it doesn't mean that your children can't be.

Crazy idea 5#: The child who does something first will be the best at it

Complete rubbish! We live in a world where childhood has been made into a race. The child who can read first, run fastest, draw best is deemed to be the one most likely to succeed. Not true. Most child prodigies do not grow up to be adult geniuses. They don't even turn into experts.

The evidence is that the reverse is true: being a bit older when you accomplish things is a stronger indicator of long-term success. Being a little bit older than your classmates at school gives you an advantage that lasts all the way through school.

Crazy idea #6: Success at school and success in life is the same thing

Success can't just be measured by school marks. Certainly the marks are helpful, but even more important is your child's interest in learning. We live in changing times where a school leaver today entering the job market can expect to have at least six career changes during their working lives. Success is not just about school marks, it's about your child's attitude to and interest in learning.

The link between school marks and success is tenuous at best. As the saying goes, 'don't peak in high school'. Most millionaires were only average students. Many Nobel Prize winners had a dreadful time at school.

Excelling at school doesn't mean you're a genius

Many of the people who we regard as geniuses did not do well at school:

- Sir Isaac Newton performed poorly at school.
- Albert Einstein failed his mathematics entrance exam.
- Winston Churchill failed one year of secondary school.
- Thomas Edison was considered inept at mathematics and a poor reader and left after three months of formal education.

A number of prominent people left school early:

- David Karp, founder of Tumblr, left at age 15

- Ray Kroc, founder of McDonald's, left at age 15
- François Pinault, one of the richest businessmen in France, left at age 11
- Quentin Tarantino, film director, left at age 15
- Vidal Sassoon, hairdresser and businessman, left at age 14
- Charles Dickens, author, left at age 12
- Coco Chanel, designer and founder of the Chanel brand, left at age 18
- Peter Jackson, film director, left at age 16
- Benjamin Franklin, founder and statesman, left at age 10
- Albert Einstein, physicist, left at age 15
- Walt Disney, entertainment mogul, left at age 16
- Richard Branson, businessman, left at age 16
- Sir Charles Mackerras, musical conductor, left at age 15
- Justice Michael McHugh, High Court judge, left at age 15
- Kathy Lette, author, left at age 15
- Paul Keating, former Australian Prime Minister, left at age 14
- Lindsay Fox, trucking tycoon, left at age 16
- Alan Sugar, business magnate, left at age 16

Many prominent people did not complete their tertiary studies either, including Bill Gates, Steve Jobs, F. Scott Fitzgerald and Mark Zuckerberg.

Creative people often do poorly at school before becoming high performers in their fields. In fact, it may be that facing some setbacks assists the development of genius. No pearl without the grit, as some might say.

Crazy idea #7: Responsible parenting is about solving problems for your children

The golden rule of parenting: Don't do things for your children that you want them to be able to do for themselves.

Many people treat parenting as if they should be Mr/Ms/Mrs Fix-it. But rushing around solving problems for your children is not going to teach them to be self-reliant. If you are going to have any chance of your children supporting you at all in your more senior years, you should start thinking about how to help them become empowered, capable creators of their own destiny.

The most prominent writers on children's development agree that challenges drive development. It is when children encounter a problem they have not faced before, an idea that doesn't fit neatly into their world or a new perspective they have not considered, it is then that they grow intellectually.

A mind that stretches itself to let a new idea in, never goes back to the same shape. As parents your role is not to solve problems for children but to pose questions, and provide opportunities to try new things out in a context of love, support and encouragement.

Let your children tackle problems: it builds their brains. Be there to support them, encourage them and cheer them on but don't solve every problem for them. Mollycoddling them, pandering to their every whim, allowing them to avoid things that make them anxious or sorting things out for them is just not helpful in the long term. Rushing up to the school to smooth over any friendship disruptions or to avoid any setbacks simply communicates to your children that you don't believe they are able to sort these things out for themselves.

Love them, support them, be there for them and always look for opportunities to build their belief in their capabilities. You don't hand children with a broken pencil a new one: you show them where a sharpener is and tell them to get to work.

Think back to when you watched your children take those first stumbling steps as they learned to walk. You didn't rush around removing every obstacle in their path. Most likely you stayed close by to make sure they didn't hurt themselves as they painstakingly moved across the room.

The parenting wisdom you used then is the same wisdom you should use to unlock their genius. *Prepare the child for the path, not the path for the child.*

Crazy idea #8: Everyone deserves a prize

I recently heard about a parent who circulated a birthday invitation to her eight-year-old daughter's friends and also requested that people bring a present for her younger brother. It was not the younger brother's birthday.

The idea that everyone should receive a prize is toxic to the development of your child's genius. Whether it is pass the parcel where everyone gets a present or sports competitions where everyone gets a trophy for participating, try to stay away from them.

In life, everyone does not get a present. There will be days when you are the birthday girl or boy and others when you are not. You won't run first in every race and if you expect to do so, the first time you lose a race you will give up running at all.

Children who come to expect and rely on praise, rewards and ribbons every time they try something give up trying as soon as the rewards dry up. For example, research shows that receiving rewards such as stickers when learning to read books makes it less likely that children will enjoy reading for its own sake.

Just turning up is not sufficient. Success and genius require people to endure setbacks and keep trying. Effort and persistence are necessary qualities.

Crazy idea #9: The modern world is good for growing genius

We live in a world that minimises play, exploration and curiosity. Often we don't give children access to smart people or ideas. Instead, we give them celebrities and pop culture.

Unlocking your child's genius involves stepping back from some of the mayhem of life. The time to explore, enjoy, think, consider, create and, most importantly, play, is sadly becoming rare in our world. In order to do this you will need to be different to many of the families around you. It will require that you step off the well-trodden path to create a path of your own.

Crazy idea #10: We should just go back to the 'good old days' and teach children the basics

The world has changed irrevocably and unrecognisably from your childhood to your children's. It was around 1995 that the world shifted in a way that was as dramatic as the shift from the Dark Ages to the Renaissance. A world without electronic connectivity, social media and the internet is simply unimaginable for many children.

Some adults become wary of new ideas that are different from the ones that were around when they grew up. While reading, writing and numeracy are always going to be important skills, there are a whole new set of thinking skills needed to develop genius in the modern world.

Closing our minds to the research and opportunities available for our children would be like going to a doctor and hearing them say, 'I've heard about those new screening tests but I'm not interested in investigating them.'

The change to a computerised world has brought much that is positive as well as some problems that are toxic. It gives our children access to vast amounts of information but also risks creating entertained, passive viewers rather than participants in life. Our task is to help our children capitalise on the positive aspects of the new world while protecting them from the negatives.

Key ways to unlock your child's genius	
Ages 2–4	<ul><li>Allow your child to play in the way that they want. At this age, many children start by looking on, then begin solitary play before shifting to some parallel play with other children; follow your child's lead.</li><li>Gently start the process of expanding rather than accelerating, point out different objects and perspectives.</li><li>Group simple shapes and colours.</li><li>Play, play and more play. When in doubt play more; it enriches minds.</li><li>Read aloud great stories and fairy tales to them, e.g. Dr. Seuss books, *The Lion, the Witch and the Wardrobe*. Some stories should involve movement and sounds; others should be read sitting quietly. Helping your child to sit quietly and listen will give them greater early experiences at school.</li><li>If grandparents are available remember they are wonderful teachers of almost everything, especially reading!</li><li>Conduct a running commentary in adult language about what you are doing with your child.</li><li>Count things: fingers, toes, ears, trees, dogs.</li><li>Help children to identify the letters of the alphabet.</li><li>Create with them cloth scrapbooks of letters and pictures of things that start with A, B through to Z.</li></ul>

	■ Use all of the senses, encourage kids to touch, smell, see, hear and even taste a variety of things
Ages 5–7	■ By these years children will be able to play collaboratively but may still choose solitary play at times. ■ Support their play by surrounding them with stimulation for the senses – pine cones, cotton wool, coloured paper, water, clay, mud, paint, acorns, buttons, ribbons, pebbles, feathers, aroma and touch. ■ Read to them and with them: picture books such as the *Just So Stories for Little Children* by Rudyard Kipling. ■ Wherever possible rather than telling kids about things, involve them in experiences; hearing about the stars at night is not as good as stargazing at night. ■ Teach them to tell the time, learn to count, draw circles and anti-clockwise circles (important for writing); sing the alphabet and times tables with them. ■ Children usually love signing their name and writing their address on envelopes; help them to send letters. Continue to create homemade cloth spelling and alphabet books. ■ Wherever possible involve children in making things. For example, rather than just looking at a clock they can make one using a paper plate or a pizza box and a straw. ■ Collect, sort and categorise things. ■ Have creativity corners in your home and expect children to get dirty. Put up a sign: 'Work in Progress' or 'Geniuses at Work – Don't interrupt'. ■ Find an old drawer with internal partitions and fill it with objects children can use in their play and paintings.

	<ul><li>Take lots of photos of your child doing things.</li><li>Don't use rewards, badges and stickers; instead reward your child with conversation and time.</li><li>Have a noticeboard at home at child level displaying a thought or question of the day.</li><li>Remind children that their brain is like a muscle that can get stronger and smarter as they use it.</li></ul>
Ages 8–11	<ul><li>Children can think in quite sophisticated ways in these years if they are guided by an adult who has a love of learning new things. In the earlier years you were following their lead, now you will use your knowledge of the world to take their interests and build on them.</li><li>Play should become more imaginative, active and exciting for children.</li><li>Remind children that their brain is like a muscle that can get stronger and smarter as they use it.</li><li>Keep building imaginative thinking by asking questions: How many uses can you think of for a …? How might … and … be similar? How might they be different?</li><li>At all ages you want children to be excited about learning. Help them to investigate ideas, plan and complete projects, and conduct experiments.</li><li>Remember you have at your fingertips the best workshop to help your child be excited about learning – it's called the world.</li><li>Use blocks, dice and tiles to help them understand numeracy.</li><li>Use shopping trips as an exercise to build numeracy skills.</li></ul>

- Make shopping lists (to build planning and budgeting skills).
- Link some of their reading to films and television shows (especially for boys).
- As well as continuing to photograph your child doing things, hand the camera over to them and ask them to take photographs or make short videos.
- Ask children to make maps, outlines, diagrams and visual to-do lists. Make signs.
- Encourage kids to do puppetry, poetry, pottery, sculpture.
- Have them learn some poems and songs by heart.
- Take children to magic shows, circuses, agricultural shows, cinemas.
- Develop numeracy by using:
  - blocks
  - card towers
  - comparing amounts
  - cooking
  - jigsaw puzzles
  - knives, forks and spoons
  - ordering, arranging counting and rearranging
  - saving up to buy something
  - shapes and colour
  - shopping
  - sorting
  - time.

| Ages 12–18 | <ul><li>This is a peak time for neuroplasticity so the experiences we can give teenagers shape their brains.</li><li>Remind them that learning and success can be cool.</li><li>Keep exposing them to different experiences and ways of viewing the world.</li><li>Use conversations over the dining room table to develop ideas and persuasive arguments.</li><li>Find connections between ideas.</li><li>As some teenagers think they know everything, keep broadening their world.</li><li>Incorporate the methods in this book on organising information and note taking so they become habitual.</li><li>Broaden their world by visiting such places as:<ul><li>agricultural shows</li><li>art galleries and exhibitions</li><li>churches, mosques, synagogues and temples</li><li>courts</li><li>farms</li><li>fire stations</li><li>historical and archaeological sites</li><li>museums</li><li>music performances including symphonic recitals</li><li>parliament</li><li>satellite stations, lighthouses, observatories, aquariums, zoos</li><li>science works</li><li>theatre.</li></ul></li></ul> |

- Develop their sense of compassion and understanding by volunteering at homeless shelters, animal refuges, refugee centres, disaster recovery places, care homes. Help them to develop the sense that they can help other people and improve the world.
- Maintain their level of physical activity by encouraging them to be involved in activities like:
  - camping
  - kite-flying
  - orienteering
  - scouts or guides
  - skateboarding
  - skiing
  - snowboarding
  - sports clubs
  - surfing
  - canoeing
  - youth clubs.
- Go on holidays and stay at youth hostels.
- Remind teens that their brain is like a muscle that can get stronger and smarter as they use it.

CHAPTER 2

The genius brain

*All children are born geniuses, and we spend the first six
years of their lives degeniusing them.*

Buckminster Fuller(4)

So if we have a world where intelligence has increased and there
are people with all this intellectual and creative capacity, why isn't
the world full of geniuses? The reason is that there are many people
who have blockages to their learning. In this chapter I discuss how
the genius brain actually works. To explain this, I need to introduce
you to Rex and Albert.

Introducing Rex and Albert

Basically, we have two brains. These were originally described
by Oliver Emberton as Rex and Albert.

The first part of our brain developed a long, long time ago and
forms the bottom part of our brain. We could talk about the reticular
activating system and the basal ganglia, but it is more fun to call
this part of the brain 'Rex'.

It's pretty much the same brain dinosaurs had and it does some
pretty nifty stuff. It keeps you alive. It keeps you breathing while
you sleep. It tells you how to wake up. It cools you down when you
overheat. It slows you down when you rush too much. Rex does a lot
of important things automatically so you don't even have to think
about them. It helps you to survive.

The Rex part of your brain is not a genius. He likes things very,
very straightforward and simple. Rex is very old, can get quite

grumpy and isn't very bright. Rex doesn't use language or logic much so he can't be reasoned with. Also he is incredibly easy to distract.

The other part of our brain is the brilliant, insightful, creative and compassionate part that has most recently developed in humans. Historically speaking it is still pretty new. It's still going through a few refinements and has some wonky patches, especially in the teen years, but as a work in progress, it's doing pretty well. Some people call it our prefrontal cortex, but for now let's call this part of our brain 'Albert'. Albert is our genius brain.

Now we all like to think that our Albert brain runs the show. We are all reasonable, intelligent people in control of our own destinies, right? Wrong! Rex runs the show. Rex will listen to Albert at times, but only if it is something Rex wants to hear. For example, your Albert might decide to go on a diet, but if your inner Rex wants to lie on the couch watching soap operas and eating chocolate cake, I'd suggest you don't approach those scales for a while yet.

If your Albert says, 'This issue isn't worth worrying about', but Rex detects threat, you're likely to be up pacing the floorboards at 4 am.

Rex has many more brain cells than Albert. In fact, Rex has about 80 per cent of all our brain cells.

Rex is incredibly distractible. Comfort matters a lot to Rex. You can get your Albert to take matters into hand but only if you distract Rex with something to keep him comfortable. Food, drink, sleep, rest and distractions all help Rex to settle for a while.

The problem for many of us is that as soon as Rex is feeling warm and snuggly we think the problem is solved and don't put our Albert to work to sort out the issue. We take a break. Things are fine, we think, and they are until our disgruntled Rex roars back to life.

Unlocking genius requires us to help our children learn something many people don't know how to do: tame Rex and activate Albert.

What happens when Rex is having a bad day

When Rex is out of sorts and detects what he perceives to be a threat we can be on a rollercoaster of emotions. One moment we can be filled with joy and pleasure and the next moment, we are argumentative and aggressive.

The problem is that Rex isn't bright enough to know the difference between real threats and imagined ones. For Rex, fearing failing a test, having to wait for lunch, not getting enough rest or being yelled at, are all threats.

Rex can get all worked up over nothing. And once he is unhappy he can stay unhappy for a while. Once revved up, Rex isn't especially good at calming down.

This is why if someone says something nasty to you, you can feel out of sorts for the whole day. When people feel the need to bully, dominate or harass other people, it is their Rex at work. When people feel that if they make a mistake it will be a disaster, it is Rex blowing it out of proportion. When children stress out about not coming first or being picked for a team, or not getting the marks they want on a test, Rex is running the show.

Developing genius requires knowing that our brain plays tricks on us at times and we all need to teach our children how to placate or distract Rex, so they can use their inner Albert.

How Rex and Albert change over time

When we are born we are pretty much all Rex. Survival is the most pressing matter after being born; lots of reaction and not too much advanced thinking happening in those really early weeks of life.

Then, kapow! The baby's brain starts to get busy. Impressively busy. While Rex is busy working out how to get some food into the mouth or how to move a thumb to suck on it, Albert is trying to work out how the world works. At first, Albert shows great interest in edges, stripes and faces.

In the first few months, while Rex is busy tinkering with the body's machinery, Albert is starting a series of scientific experiments that will continue throughout life. By around eight months of age, Albert has worked out that if Mum puts on her coat she might be going out and so tries to find out what crying will make her do.

Around two years of age, language gives Albert a boost. Children now start playing make-believe games, using their imagination and being able to think about ideas as well as actions. Language allows them to make meaning.

Albert, the budding young scientist, develops increasingly intricate experiments to learn how the world works using his or her favourite lab rats; parents and grandparents. By three or four years of age, many of these experiments involve finding out 'what will they do if I scream loudly enough'.

During childhood the brain develops an enormous number of connections (called synapses) between brain cells. At birth, children have about 2500 synapses per brain cell. By their third birthday they have 15,000 connections between each brain cell.

As bright as kids naturally are, the budding genius has a few limitations. Albert is still fairly rigid and focused on the appearance of things. Organising and sorting is a challenge. Understanding is heavily based on experience so abstract ideas such as considering consequences, weighing up different points of view and considering peoples' intentions when judging actions are not really well thought through. There is also a lot of wonderful magical thinking. Inanimate things such as clouds and rocks have feelings.

Around seven years of age Albert becomes more flexible and less centred on one point of view. It is often at this time that comparisons between a child's own performance and that of other people can start creating anxiety.

Around eight or nine years of age, the brain has more connections than it needs and so it begins a process known as 'synaptic pruning'. This affects Albert more than Rex. Thinking styles and processes change. The brain starts to do away with those connections it doesn't use. Partly, it is this process that allows humans to specifically shape their behaviour to their environments.

During these years, the brain starts to slow down. A seven-year-old's brain runs at about twice the speed that yours does, and between eight and eighteen it slows down to its adult running rate.

From the age of nine years on, the motto for the brain should be, 'use it or lose it!' This is why the experiences we give children and young people between their ninth and eighteenth years are so important. What parents do with their children in this time has a major influence in shaping and developing Albert.

Parents and teachers are neuro-architects

Our brains mature from the bottom towards the top and from the right to the left. This means that for most children, they will make sense of their experiences before they will be fully able to express in words their ideas or feelings about an experience.

Throughout a child's development, interactions with parents and teachers shape the structures of the brain. Having parents who are calming, loving and soothing means that Rex does not become too fussed over things. Having parents who guide and inspire, who expose children to new ideas and experiences, unlocks Albert.

Between seven and eleven years of age, children enter a stage that Jean Piaget called 'concrete operations'. What this means is that while they are not ready to think in highly sophisticated ways, they are not far off either. In fact, if a child has an adult who points out different perspectives, ways of viewing things or ways of thinking about something, they can grasp quite intricate ideas.

Albert undergoes a major renovation from about the age of eight or nine. This is the start of the teen brain. As many as 30,000 synapses may be lost per second in the early adolescent brain, leading to an ultimate loss of almost half of the synapses that were present in childhood. The half that is left is why the skills we learned in childhood tend to stay with us throughout life.

At this time, Albert is restructuring to become more clever and more efficient. It is important to capitalise on this by helping young people create patterns of thinking and habits of learning that are productive. By doing this we put into place trajectories of thinking and learning that lead to future success.

In a teenager's brain, Albert, also known as the frontal lobes – the part that helps us to plan, consider, control impulses and make wise judgements – is the last bit to mature. Someone probably should put a sign on the frontal lobes of most early adolescents saying 'Closed for Construction'.

If you ever really want to lose weight, it's easy: put your teenagers in charge of preparing all your meals. I doubt you'll starve to death but I wouldn't suggest you'd get a steady supply of food either.

So, what's the big deal with the frontal lobes? It's really the frontal lobes that allow us to be civilised and human. Susan Greenfield estimates that over the course of history the size of frontal lobes in humans has increased by 29 per cent compared with chimpanzees' frontal lobes, which have increased by 17 per cent and cats, whose frontal lobes have only grown by 3 per cent.

This not only tells you a lot about why a hungry cat won't leave well enough alone, it should give you pause to think compassionately about your ancestors, who had to spend their lives hanging around with a group of eternally impulsive and erratic teenagers of various species while working out a way to produce evolution's latest upgrade – you! I hope you are duly grateful.

So in early adolescence Albert has essentially gone missing in action for a time. He is in major refit mode. This means that teenagers' brains are all tuned up for Rex-like emotions like fighting, running away and romance, but not so well tuned up for the Albert skills of planning, controlling impulses and forward thinking.

Some parents forget that while many teens look big and mature, their brains are works in progress. Parents who wouldn't dream of giving their teenager free access to their life savings can leave them in charge of a £300,000 house full of fine furniture and still be stunned by the results!

How Rex and Albert fight one another

Rex and Albert at times go to war against each other. Rex wants an easy and untroubled life. Rex doesn't like change and wants to get things back to living the easy life as quickly as possible. Albert, on the other hand, is insatiably curious and wants to think about things in new and exciting ways.

Learning is all about taking on new ideas and information and using these to change the way we think in the future. Rex likes the automatic habitual ways of doing things while Albert likes innovative new ways.

Rex is our default mode. If we get tired, overwhelmed, anxious or disheartened by the challenges ahead we retreat back into the old safe ways. Rex is very important in keeping us alive, but if Rex is too prominent in a child's life, it is very hard for the genius Albert to emerge.

See Chapter 9, 'Building a can-do mindset: The psychology of genius', for more on helping your child sort out Rex and Albert thoughts. If you are interested in immediate things you can do to soothe and calm your child's Rex, see Chapters 13 and 14.

Ways to tame Rex	
Ensure that ...	**Avoid ...**
The family eats a healthy diet: e.g. takeaway food only once a month; eat more vegetables and fruit; avoid soft drinks.	Family conflict.
You tell your children that you love them.	Talking about world troubles negatively in front of children.
You show interest in new ideas.	Discussing money problems in front of children.
Attempts at something new are encouraged and mistakes are allowed.	Physical punishment.
Children have good, consistent sleep patterns.	Negative comments about the other parent in separated families.
Little kids (and sometimes big ones) have naps.	Negative comments about school or teachers.
You encourage physical activity and sports.	Ridicule, sarcasm or comments that could create shame.
You take family walks – change the scenery or the context.	Saying, 'Well, I was never much good at that either ...'
You convey a sense that you believe in your child and that problems can be overcome.	Yelling or threatening.

Once Rex is not so much of an issue for your child read on as we start to discover ways to develop Albert. Given that experiences are so important in allowing genius to flourish, I've given you below a starter kit of ideas to plan to do with your child that will help Albert come to the fore.

You might like to tick those that you have already done and place an asterisk next to those you plan to do in the near future.

Genius-building and mind-stretching experiences for children	
Ages 2–4	■ Blow and catch bubbles.
	■ Visit a farm.
	■ Ride a mini steam train.
	■ Build something out of blocks.
	■ Spin a top.
	■ Dance.
	■ Gaze at clouds and find shapes.
	■ Play racing cars in a cardboard box.
	■ Play in the bathtub or in a cardboard box.
	■ Dress up.
	■ Play in a sandpit and make mud pies.
	■ Explore rock pools.
	■ Visit a circus.
	■ Pat a pet.
	■ Help in the garden.
	■ Sing songs.
	■ Bounce on a bouncy castle.
	■ Start to learn to swim.
	■ Run, jump and skip.
	■ Finger paint.

	■ Make a sandcastle or snowman. ■ Drum. ■ Play with puppets and dolls. ■ Count fingers and toes. ■ Spend time with grandparents. ■ Ride a tricycle. ■ Get pushed in a soapbox car. ■ Slide down a slide. ■ Sort shapes and colours. ■ Look at and make paintings and art works. ■ Memorise short funny poems and rhymes. ■ Sing 'Old MacDonald Had a Farm'. ■ Paint at an easel. ■ Play the kazoo.
Ages 5–7	■ Use an old cardboard box as an indoor slide. ■ Cut a pool noodle in half to create a marble race track. ■ Learn to skip, ride a bike, fly a kite or bounce a ball. ■ Visit a zoo. ■ Paint, knit or make a clay pot. ■ Play cards, tell a joke, have conversations. ■ Donate time to a charity. ■ Make a hat out of newspaper. ■ Learn to tie shoelaces, and click their fingers. ■ Milk a cow or goat. ■ Throw and catch a frisbee. ■ Toss a coin. ■ Care for a pet. ■ Shuffle cards. ■ Play Monopoly. ■ Balance on a fence.

	<ul><li>Look through the cracks of a pier.</li><li>Draw a cartoon.</li><li>Build a soapbox car.</li><li>Create some wild art.</li><li>Play Pooh sticks.</li><li>Set up a snail race.</li><li>Jump over waves.</li><li>Pick blackberries.</li><li>Explore inside a tree.</li><li>Go stargazing.</li><li>Explore a cave.</li><li>Hunt for bugs.</li><li>Catch a falling leaf.</li></ul>
Ages 8–11	<ul><li>Play balloon ping pong.</li><li>Play a bowling game with pencil erasers and marbles.</li><li>Hold an Olympics competition.</li><li>Throw a boomerang.</li><li>Somersault.</li><li>Create a 'shop' in the street.</li><li>Learn to juggle.</li><li>Go on a walk barefoot.</li><li>Roll down a big slope.</li><li>Run around in the rain.</li><li>Fly a kite.</li><li>Make mud pies.</li><li>Build a bonfire.</li><li>Make a tent indoors from a blanket and a table.</li><li>Go camping indoors.</li><li>Create a walkie-talkie.</li><li>Make and ride a go-cart.</li></ul>

- Dam a stream.
- Build a sandcastle.
- Play in the snow.
- Make a daisy chain.
- Make a home for a wild animal.
- Investigate rock pools.
- Go snorkelling.
- Catch a crab.
- Plant it, grow it, eat it.
- Go swimming in the sea.
- Hold a space rock.
- Feel a fossil.
- Visit a zoo, art gallery, museum, planetarium.
- Make a present for someone.
- Draw a map.
- Play the harmonica.
- Play with a remote control plane or boat.
- Learn a magic trick.
- Jump on a trampoline.
- Play ping pong.
- Chase the end of a rainbow
- Search for hidden treasure
- Play with sparklers in the dark.
- Learn a magic trick.
- Have a slumber party.
- Go on a night hunt.
- Look at the world through a microscope, telescope or kaleidoscope.
- Experiment with a chemistry set.
- Play a phonograph.

	▪ Ride a horse. ▪ Make paper planes. ▪ Visit underground caves. ▪ Make a sculpture out of junk. ▪ Visit a tip. ▪ Keep silk worms. ▪ Look after an ant colony. ▪ Be a pirate. ▪ Visit a church, synagogue, mosque. ▪ Visit historical sites especially those offering re-enactments. ▪ Attend an air show.
Ages 12–18	▪ Create your own t-shirt designs. ▪ Learn how to tie-dye. ▪ Do origami. ▪ Create a crystal radio. ▪ Braid hair. ▪ Play Twister. ▪ Go to an auction. ▪ Develop a negative photograph. ▪ Go on a wilderness hike. ▪ Go indoor rock climbing. ▪ Play volleyball. ▪ Find your way using a map and a compass. ▪ Canoe down a river. ▪ Volunteer to help a social service. ▪ Sing in a choir. ▪ Go on a long bike ride. ▪ Build a den. ▪ Climb a tree.

- Cook on a campfire.
- Hunt for fossils or bones.
- Discover what is in a pond.
- Track wild animals.
- Hold a scary creature.
- Go birdwatching.
- Camp out in the wild.
- Catch a fish.
- Eat fruit straight from a tree.
- Skim a stone.
- Make a trail with sticks.
- Go out dancing.
- Build a raft.
- Try outdoor rock climbing.
- Climb a large hill.
- Find a geocache.
- Have a candlelit dinner.
- Cook a multiple course meal.
- Handle a bank account.
- Shop and budget and save up.
- Learn to drive a car.
- Have a real or mock share portfolio and learn about the stock market.
- Sell something at a market.
- Sell something on eBay.
- Help at an archaeological dig.
- Conduct a biological survey of flora and fauna.
- Visit an art exhibition.
- Write poetry.
- Write a song.

CHAPTER 3

Identifying your child's genius

The man who achieves makes many mistakes, but he never makes the biggest mistake of all – doing nothing.

Benjamin Franklin

To unlock your child's genius you need to work out what he or she is already good at. Building on strengths goes a lot further than remedying weaknesses.

Intelligence quotients are derived from measuring many areas of ability. The old idea that there is a general factor that predicts how clever you are has really been surpassed. Many researchers who work in this field, including David Wechsler and Howard Gardner, argue that there are different types of intelligences. Some people have a very even scatter of capacities while others have what are referred to as 'splinter' skills; they may be average in quite a few areas but have exceptional potential in one or two areas.

You don't need to be good at everything

The good news about the idea of different areas of intelligence is that you don't need to be a genius in every area. Geniuses aren't usually all-rounders. Mozart wasn't a great ice hockey player, Marie Curie couldn't play cricket to save herself and Leonardo Da Vinci was a miserable table tennis partner.

To develop genius you need to know what your child is good at and amplify those strengths. To use our earlier analogy, we need to find out what is in each child's glass and make more of it.

What we can learn from David and Goliath

Underdogs can win but they need to play to their own strengths. History is replete with examples of the non-fancied side toppling the favourite against the odds.

The trend is usually for fancied favourites to defeat underdogs. Usually the stronger team or opponent defeats the weaker opponent on 71.5 per cent of occasions according to political scientist Ivan Arreguín-Toft.

You probably recall the story of David and the much bigger and stronger Goliath. When David was preparing to go into battle with Goliath he put on a helmet, some armour and grabbed a sword. Then he decided to use his speed and accuracy rather than his strength against Goliath. David picked up his slingshot and five stones instead.

When the Goliaths of this world show up, as Goliaths inevitably do, most people don't know how to shift their game plan and play to their strengths simply because they don't know what their personal strengths are.

But! When the Davids of this world understand their strengths and play to them, their winning rate goes up from 28.5 per cent of the time to 63.6 per cent on the majority of occasions.

Map your child's smarts with the pizza smarts chart

Your child's intelligence is like a supreme pizza with different flavours on different slices. Some slices are large and bursting with ingredients while other slices have hardly any bits on them at all. This is true for most of us.

The idea that we all have different types of intelligence is not so surprising when you look at the world around us. There are dancers who you wouldn't want running your accounts; there are bankers who should stay well away from karaoke bars.

Knowing your child's strengths and building on them is an essential step in unlocking their genius. An easy way to begin identifying your child's strengths is with a pizza smarts chart. The example chart on the next page shows a faint outline of a pizza divided into ten different slices, with each slice representing a different type of intelligence. The different types of smarts are:

Number smart: Working with mathematics and numbers and calculations.

Word smart: Reading, writing, spelling.

Logic smart: Thinking issues through and clearly coming to a conclusion.

Picture smart: Art, design, construction, mechanics.

Technology smart: Computers, using tools to create things, video making.

Body smart: Fitness, health, strength, healing and acting.

Nature smart: Farming, caring for animals, looking after the environment.

Music smart: Playing, creating, listening to or singing music.

People smart: Understanding others, creating friendships, resolving differences, managing, inspiring and connecting with other people.

Self smart: Perhaps the most important smart of all; knowing yourself, your likes, dislikes, your areas of strength and interests.

Draw the outline of the shape of your child's pizza (i.e. genius). Older children and teenagers can do this for themselves.

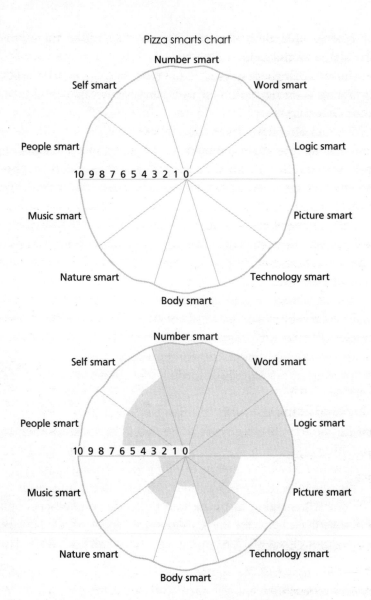

In the example above, the person regards themselves as very number, word and logic smart (pizza slice filled to the edge of the line) but less smart in other areas.

Most people have never mapped their strengths. By outlining the shape of children's pizza smarts, you are in a more powerful position to help them to learn their strengths and to build on them.

You may also want to draw a second line to indicate the areas your child enjoys.

Parents are often in the most powerful position to help their children discover their strengths and in the process enable their genius to flourish. By focusing some of your energies on exposing your child to experiences that expand existing areas of strength you build confidence and a willingness to try new things in your child.

The one thing we can reliably predict about the future is that it will change. This means that children who are equipped to take on changes rather than being intimidated by them will be the geniuses of the 21st century.

In the following chapters I discuss ways to build the skills that will unlock your child's genius. In order to guide you, you may wish to rate their current level of competence in the following areas.

	no skills									mastery
Concentration	0	1	2	3	4	5	6	7	8	9	10
Clarity of thinking	0	1	2	3	4	5	6	7	8	9	10
Planning	0	1	2	3	4	5	6	7	8	9	10
Decision-making	0	1	2	3	4	5	6	7	8	9	10
Motivation	0	1	2	3	4	5	6	7	8	9	10
Persistence	0	1	2	3	4	5	6	7	8	9	10
Creativity	0	1	2	3	4	5	6	7	8	9	10
Organisational skills	0	1	2	3	4	5	6	7	8	9	10
Memory	0	1	2	3	4	5	6	7	8	9	10
Ability to practise	0	1	2	3	4	5	6	7	8	9	10
Family routines that support learning	0	1	2	3	4	5	6	7	8	9	10

It can be useful to come back to these ratings from time to time as it will help you to see the progress your child has made as well as thinking about what strengths they can capitalise on.

Ways to identify your child's strengths
Ages 2–4 <ul><li>Guide children through a variety of experiences so they can start to develop a basis of life experience to develop strengths.</li><li>Broaden your child's range of experiences.</li><li>Let them play and get dirty.</li><li>At each stage of life, you will need to observe, reconsider and re-learn your child's strengths. Some fledgling strengths will flourish while others will dwindle. Don't be concerned at this unfolding process – it is your child's way of becoming their own unique self.</li><li>Playfully follow your child's lead. Let them explore and discover the world and themselves.</li><li>The idea is to expand their experiences rather than to accelerate them.</li></ul>
Ages 5–7 <ul><li>As a parent you may start to form a few ideas about their strengths, but don't get too prescriptive.</li><li>Do map out the pizza smarts but use it as a rough progress map rather than as an indication of future areas of strength.</li><li>During these years children can be like Toad of Toad Hall, taking up new interests with gusto only to be dismissive of them weeks later. Don't be perturbed. This experimental trying-out and sifting of experiences adds to their 'experience bank account'.</li></ul>

	• Eventually you will want children to stick with things but don't get too worried about their persistence at this stage. • The emphasis should be on broadening their range of interests rather than rushing them from one class to another.
Ages 8–11	• Often this is the first time parents will be able to confidently draw the pizza smarts chart; use this knowledge to build your child's confidence and self-belief. • Focus on a few main areas but still be prepared to give your child time to explore new skills and activities. • Interests and passions may surge according to friendships and fashion. That's fine, but keep looking beyond this to the activities your child keeps coming back to. Encourage them to develop a few areas they feel passionately about and give them the opportunity to develop some expertise in these areas.
Ages 12–18	• The teen years can either be a time when the strengths are crystal clear to parents or when new areas of strength emerge as children mature. • Complete the pizza smarts chart annually. • Changing schools can be an opportunity for expansion of strength areas. • Some teens need to keep their areas of passion secret from their friends. Protect and guard their privacy. Embarrassment can extinguish a passion easily at this age.

- The teen years are often a quest for belonging. By identifying strength areas you can help them to:
  - find people and places that value their attributes and what they have to offer.
  - stay away from people and places who do not value what they have to offer.
- Encourage volunteering experiences.
- Work placements and part-time jobs are good ways to build on an interest.
- For teens who find it difficult to see their own strengths, it may be useful to consider adding to the pizza smarts, by mapping strengths, career testing or intelligence testing.

CHAPTER 4

Increasing concentration skills

'How come I have to pay for attention?'

Question asked by eight-year-old boy
after being told at school to sit down and pay attention

Let's now turn our thoughts to how building on a child's strengths can be used to increase a skill that underpins all acts of genius: the ability to concentrate.

The concentration span of most kids is at least a rainy day of reruns of *The Simpsons* and *Family Guy*, ten consecutive games of Call of Duty, viewing the postings from 400 Facebook friends, 60 texts from besties, and a whole day of nagging you for something they really, really want.

The ability of kids to concentrate is not the problem: the issue is how to help them to fix their focus on one thing and keep it there. As the world becomes more complex, the ability to hold sustained concentration to think deeply about ideas is a distinguishing feature of genius.

This is partly because brains are wired to wander. Rex likes to prowl around amusing and distracting himself. The advent of multitasking plays into our natural tendencies of directing our attention to the latest and the greatest. Concentration is a limited resource. We only have so much focus before our mind starts to wander off in search of new entertainment. Paying attention to one thing necessarily comes at the expense of another.

Everyone has concentration problems from time to time. Especially when our primitive brain becomes overloaded, tired, hungry, sleep-deprived or anxious. To ensure that we sustain our concentration we need to take Rex out of the equation. We can do this by developing systems, checklists, procedures, formulas and habits.

The amount of learning children can do directly relates to their ability to concentrate and focus attention. Many of history's recognised geniuses were known to have tenacious levels of concentration. Einstein, Newton and Darwin were all noted for their ability to concentrate. Thomas Edison performed 1600 experiments in an attempt to find the most suitable filament for a light bulb. Of course, being so focused can also have its downside: Edison became so lost in his experiments he forgot to attend his own wedding. On one occasion Albert Einstein and a geologist friend were so engrossed in a discussion about earthquakes that neither noticed a big earthquake was actually happening and their building had been evacuated.

Geniuses develop laser-like levels of concentration for the things they are interested in. Sometimes they also have scant disregard for almost everything else. Isaac Newton only realised he was boiling his watch when he tried to tell the time by looking at an egg.

Has anyone ever said to you, 'You've got a mind like a sieve?' Well, they were right! Approximately 99 per cent of the information that comes into your awareness is immediately discarded. That's just as well because if it wasn't, you would be swamped with trivial detail. Thankfully, you are a very discerning person. When you were a kid, however, you weren't quite so discerning.

Concentration is a bit like a bouncer at a nightclub. It rapidly inspects candidates – in this case ideas – for admission to the brain and filters out and discards those it thinks are unworthy of further attention. Some children have a bouncer that lets in too many ideas; others the wrong sort. So the trick to developing genius levels of concentration in children is for them to learn what to concentrate on and what to filter out.

Most of us are skilled at screening out irrelevant information. For example, most of you will not have been aware of your shoes on your feet until your attention is drawn to them. Children are often less skilled at working out what is the main thing to concentrate on.

Developing concentration

Like any other skill, concentration can be enhanced and made more automatic. Anyone who has learned a complex set of manoeuvres – such as riding a bike, playing a musical instrument or driving a car – will have experienced the initial concern of 'how do I concentrate on all these things at once?' only to find with practice they become easier.

Geniuses can concentrate but they focus on very specific things. In my experience children are naturally drawn towards some areas and can concentrate on them better than others. Dr Mel Levine, the author of *A Mind at a Time*, influenced much of my thinking in this area and says that we need to think about how to parent a diverse range of minds.

In following sections I discuss some common types of budding geniuses who have some interesting concentration styles. While these are general categories, they can help you to find ways to help your children focus and concentrate.

You may not be able to identify just one exact category for your children, but parents generally find it is a useful guide in helping children focus their attention when they are learning something new.

The Happy Wanderers

The area these geniuses concentrate on is visual. These are the sorts of children who may not be able to tell you what you were talking about a minute ago, but will notice that you have different shoes on today.

These children often have an amazing amount of interest and energy. It's almost as if their heads spin around trying to take everything in. Their eyes almost bounce around in their heads seeking out all sorts of things to look at or to wander over to check out. They know what they are interested in – everything they see! This can mean all visuals – colours, shapes, movement and art. If you don't capture Happy Wanderers' interest visually, they will wander off and find something else to look at. Basically if it's not visually interesting, it's not interesting.

I see... I see... I see...

One Happy Wanderer I worked with could never tell me what we had just discussed but could tell me there was a frog outside on a branch and that the left corner of the curtains was more faded than the rest.

The upside of this is that these children grow into people who are often popular, aesthetic, interesting, energetic and sensitive to the needs of others.

Happy Wanderers are often very astute at reading the emotions of other people. They are often extremely successful long term in careers that require these skills such as counselling, art collecting, business, hospitality and hotel management, as well as social work, medicine and teaching.

How you can help Happy Wanderers

To help Happy Wanderers unlock their genius you need to help them prime their concentration.

These children need visual signals that tell them it's time to listen. School teachers often use these signals – hands on hips, one finger over your lips (sssh time), hands on heads or one raised arm – to settle classrooms of kids. Parents can use these same signals at home. Maintain eye contact and reduce visual distractibility.

If you don't have eye contact with a Happy Wanderer, you don't have their attention. With smaller Wanderers, bend down and look at them *eye to eye* before trying to give them information.

Happy Wanderers are often quite cheery kids who can laugh at themselves when you bring them back on track. However, just because they respond amiably doesn't always mean they will stay on track.

These children often thrive and concentrate best in visually rich environments and can focus incredibly well if involved in producing collages, drawings, posters and flow diagrams.

Parents can help Happy Wanderers to concentrate by using:

- jigsaw puzzles – increases motor skills, abstract reasoning and spatial organisation
- I-spy games – to develop language and attention
- collages, flow charts and posters – assists planning and organising information
- coloured pieces of paper for them to write on – assists memory
- mobiles showing important photos attached to ceilings – reminds them of past successes

- glitter pens, paints and crayons – makes note-taking exciting
- the card game, concentration – for memory
- hands-on, concrete examples and diagrams in mathematics
- wall charts and timelines featuring key historical events with pictures of key people
- mind maps and brain bubble maps
- signs and reminders such as 'Pack your lunch!' on doors, refrigerators, in lunch boxes or on phones
- cue cards, palm cards (see Chapter 11 for a description of how to use these)
- spot-the-difference pictures, TED-Ed videos and animations.

The Frequent Flyers

The genius of Frequent Flyers is their ability to link seemingly unconnected ideas and concepts together with great creativity and originality. These children have ideas that ricochet around and go zooming off to distant planets and it's hard to keep their ideas in check long enough for them to focus.

Frequent flyers are creative linkers of ideas and often thrive in the long term in careers that involve these skills: marketing, scriptwriting, advertising, designing, innovative technologies, inventing and events promoting.

While these kids often grow up to be creative and imaginative adults who are innovative thinkers, they need to learn to balance their dream time with their focus time. Say to them, 'You have five minutes of dream time then we'll do five minutes of focusing.'

As their ideas bounce around at a great rate, these kids often respond to time challenges and games. For example, you can challenge them to a shopping game where they have to collect and put three items from the supermarket list into the shopping trolley before you get a set number of items.

Some Frequent Flyers get jumbled. In their rush towards the next big idea, they lose sight of the steps involved in getting there. So while routines are not Frequent Flyers' strongest suit, they will benefit from habits and routines that teach them timing and sequencing. Along with concentration and memory, the ability to put things in order (or sequencing) is a very important skill for the development of their genius.

How you can help Frequent Flyers

Parents can develop a Frequent Flyer's ability to concentrate through basic tasks like tidying up, cooking and getting ready for the day. Setting the table can be useful in developing concentration. Help them by asking questions such as: How many people are dining? How many knives will we need? Are we having soup? Do you think we should put out the plates before the place mats? Try to get them to sequence the process.

Cooking and following recipes is terrific for Frequent Flyers as it gives them a sense of sequences. Don't worry if you have a few cooking disasters – learning to put the eggs into the cake before icing it is a valuable lesson. Drama, theatre and debating are also helpful for learning sequencing. Be sure to read the section on developing systems in Chapter 8 as it strongly applies to Frequent Flyers.

Take Frequent Flyers on a mental trip where they can fancifully dream up all sorts of ideas related to a particular concept. For example, one game you can play with Frequent Flyers is to get them to dream up all the weirdest types of cars (or houses, or animals) that they can think of and talk about all of the features they like. You can then ask them to select a combination of features and draw or design one of them. This helps Frequent Flyers to learn how to value their creativity as well as how to use it.

You can help Frequent Flyers develop sequencing skills by playing:

- Battleships – assists sequencing
- chess – helps problem-solving and strategic thinking
- Chinese chequers – helps planning and identifying patterns
- ordering and arranging collections – assists sequencing
- dominoes – helps planning and sequencing
- tennis, badminton, ping pong, lacrosse, hockey, football, calisthenics, dressage – builds sequencing skills.

The Spies

These are the kids that intelligence agencies should recruit. Their genius is their ability to pick up on every word, sound, nuance and tone. You'll know if you have one of these children in your home because it's virtually impossible to have a private discussion without them picking up on it.

Spies are easily distracted by sounds. At times all the wrong sounds seem to be amplified in their minds. As they are sensitive to distracting sounds, they need to learn to reduce their exposure to them. For that reason, sitting closer to teachers is important.

Often these kids respond well to music playing softly in the background when they are learning. Headphones with soft ambient music can help them focus. Spies may learn best when you use a particular background piece of classical or instrumental music.

Experiment to see what suits your child best.

These children also learn well through sound. Audio books on CD or an iPod are good. Helping them make audio recordings of things they want to remember and using rhymes for sequences is also valuable.

Reading 'create your own adventure' books to them so they need to listen carefully and then choose a course of action can be helpful.

Some of these kids are terrific listeners. They are just not always sure what they should be listening to. Long term, many of them find successful careers as language teachers, interpreters, radio announcers, musicians, audio technicians, recording engineers, actors, telephone call-centre workers and air-traffic controllers.

Teaching Spies to listen carefully and to speak in whole sentences rather than snippets of phrases is important. Two family rules that are especially useful if you have a Spy are:

1   It's good manners to listen when someone is speaking.
2   In this family we speak in whole sentences (we don't respond, in fact we are stone deaf, to grunts, whats, dunnos, as ifs and whatevers!).

How you can help Spies

While sound is the area of genius for Spies, some are not always great listeners. They can be so quick to pick up on sounds that they find it difficult to work out which sound to focus on.

Teaching listening skills takes time and persistence (not to mention the patience of a saint!). Try using an activity where you can give instructions (such as bedtime, washing up, cleaning up the bedroom). Choose an activity later in the day so you don't have the time pressure of needing to be somewhere by a specific time.

Allow yourself enough time and don't get interrupted. Switch the phone off. Get your child's attention. Gain and maintain eye contact. Calmly ask him or her to do the task. Use brief sentences. Ladders of understanding – where you outline five steps to complete a task (see Chapter 11) – can be helpful for Spies.

Make sure they know what to do. Don't let Spies get off task. Calmly, point out the consequences if they don't do the task. Persist until the task is completed. Make a plan to help your children build this into a habit. Remember, new habits take time to learn.

You can also help Spies develop their genius by:

- having some periods of learning in silence
- using soft gentle music to lower their levels of energy
- playing rhyming games and reciting poetry
- playing 20-question games
- listening to recorded stories and audio books
- making podcasts
- playing 'repeat after me'
- playing Pictionary
- playing 'Simon says'
- summarising a sports broadcast into a highlights summary of 50 words or less
- creating newspaper headlines of the main things they need to remember.

The Fidgeters

These are the busy fingers brigade, who are always touching, fiddling, doodling, feeling, twisting and picking away at something. Their fingers are always doing something. Their genius is in their touch.

Some Fidgeters find it very difficult to focus on what is being said to them unless they are doing something with their hands. You'll find adult Fidgeters in lectures knitting, crocheting or doodling.

Fidgeters have tactile distractibility. They're the sort of kid who sits in school, not saying a word, as they become absorbed in twisting their hair. Schools often have these kids sit on physio balls or blow-up seats so that they can squirm and move while working.

These kids are often great collectors of things: bottle tops, stamps, dolls, war gaming-figures, football cards, Lego pieces, cuddly toys, golf balls, marbles and, sometimes, worms. You will find all sorts of weird things they have picked up in their pockets.

It is through arranging their collections that these children learn sequencing and develop concentration. Their bedrooms often contain a growing menagerie of objects. It's almost as if all of the genius of these kids is from their elbows down.

When they grow up Fidgeters often become skilled artists, builders, surgeons, mechanics, electricians, musicians, plumbers, carpenters, farmers, computer technicians, fashion designers, physiotherapists, masseurs or robotics technicians. It's a hands-on world for these children. They have fine motor skills to a degree that leaves the rest of us feeling clumsy and oafish.

These kids are often sensitive people who read feelings well, have excellent eye–hand and fine motor coordination.

How you can help Fidgeters

Unlocking a Fidgeter's genius is a very hands-on process for parents. Involving children in caring for pets and learning chess and musical instruments can be helpful.

Some of these children are insatiable in terms of acquisitions (this often develops into ambition!). Helping them to build collections can be worthwhile. Some Fidgeters, when they become insatiable in their demands, can be helped to focus on adding to their less expensive rock, stick, stamp, miniature figures or pressed flower collection.

Lego, building models, learning knitting or sewing, meccano sets, jigsaw puzzles, Rubik's cubes, mazes, constructing and painting small figures are just some of the activities that often help the Fidgeters to learn how to concentrate.

As these kids are often wrigglers who squirm, doodle, pick, flick and twist, teach them stillness if you can, but realise some of them just concentrate best when they are fiddling with something.

Being able to sit still is an important skill for school. Games like statues, Twister and musical chairs where you lose the chair if you get up, can assist the development of concentration and stillness. Asking your children to count how long they can hold a statue position can also be fun.

Combining actions with storytelling can be another great way of involving Fidgeters. For example, parents can say to Fidgeters that every time they hear a word in a story that is something they could drink (or eat, or jump over and so on), they can wave their hands in the air.

As with the Happy Wanderers, signals such as hands on heads or placing your fingers against your lips to indicate the desire for quietness to show that it's time to concentrate can be helpful.

Some Fidgeters are so intent on tactile sensations that you need to rev them up before teaching them stillness. Alternating times of intense activity with times of rest helps these kids to learn how to surf their energy waves and settle down.

Some Fidgeters are good at using their large muscle groups but need help to develop fine motor skills. You can help them by shifting gradually to more precise use of their muscles. For example, as well as dancing, bouncing and jumping they might be helped to start drawing, painting, shaping clay or creating craft pieces.

Activities that you can use to help your Fidgeters flourish include:

- handball – increases eye-motor coordination and team skills (especially for doubles)
- kite building and flying – encourages experimentation
- Lego – increases gross and fine motor coordination
- mazes – encourages problem-solving
- gymnastics and dance – directs energy, encourages focusing and fine and gross motor coordination
- pony clubs – increases organisation, physical strength and coordination, planning and sequencing
- musical instruments like violin, guitar, piano, cello or trumpet for those Fidgeters with fine motor skills; drums and trombones for those with strengths in gross motor skills
- model building – increases fine motor skills
- blocks, dice and tiles – helps to learn mathematics
- knitting, sewing – assists in sequencing
- woodwork – helps in planning, sequencing
- construction projects – increases skills in time management and sequencing.

The Star Trekkers

Creative brain leaps are the spark of genius in Star Trekkers. These children go where no-one has gone before! They are often inventive, exciting people who strike out in new and interesting ways towards as yet unimagined frontiers.

The absentminded professor is an example of a Star Trekker. Star Trekkers often have splinter skills with some areas being highly developed while others seem almost non-existent. They often show flashes of lightning brilliance followed by a display of vagueness.

Star Trekkers are the sort of people who may invent a whole new way of transporting people to where they want to go, but are almost incapable of dressing themselves in the morning.

When introduced to a new idea or concept they look blankly at you as if the idea has appeared mysteriously from the outer reaches of space and has no relationship to any other idea they have ever encountered. They can treat every event in their life as unique and unconnected to anything in the past.

While their apparent inability to draw upon their past learning and experience can be frustrating, these kids are often quick and exciting thinkers who are able to see new possibilities in things (partly because they are not so constrained by past thinking).

Paradoxically they can creatively connect ideas in unpredictable and creative ways, similar to the Frequent Flyers, but they overlook the obvious links right under their noses.

How you can help Star Trekkers

To unlock Star Trekkers' genius you need to help them build on their capacity to see patterns and connections. Telling them clearly how one thing connects to another is helpful, as is pointing out similarities by asking questions such as 'How are a cat and a tiger alike?' 'What do a robot and a car have in common?'

Parenting one of these kids means that you become a specialist in POTBO (pointing out the bleeding obvious) because if you don't do it, they'll never get it.

Finding ways to connect life events also helps Star Trekkers to concentrate. Calendars, diaries, posters, fridge magnets, family noticeboards and stickers are useful ways of connecting life events and developing awareness.

Life calendars are a great way of collecting memories – the family collects pictures of all the good things that have happened in January, February, on a holiday and so on and makes a collage that can be kept on the fridge as a reminder to Star Trekkers of all the good things in life. Life calendars can be used with all children.

Young Star Trekkers can benefit from routines that help them organise their thoughts. A family noticeboard that puts up highlights for each day is one method. Each day can be described in a different way – Marvellous Monday, Terrific Tuesday, Wonderful Wednesday, Tremendous Thursday, Fantastic Friday, Sensational Saturday, Superb Sunday.

Using visual aids such as stickers and reminders that it is 'x sleeps to go' before an event helps these kids to focus. (See also the homework strategies outlined in the next section for Social Secretaries.)

Older children benefit from flow charts, timelines, mind maps, diagrammatic representations and just chatting about how events relate to each other. Rule books that summarise key rules (such as 'i before e except after c') can also help them to discern patterns. In secondary school, it's important for parents to read their children's set novels because your ability to draw out connections for them will be a strong factor in their success.

If this sounds familiar to you, be sure to read closely Chapters 6 and 7 on planning and decision-making.

Jousting January	Fabulous February	Miraculous March	Awesome April
Mirthful May	Joyful June	Jingling July	Artful August
Super September	Original October	Neat November	Dynamic December

The Social Secretaries

The world of people, feelings and sharing is the area of genius for Social Secretaries. Teachers know these children well. They love people. They chatter in class. They pass notes. They send text messages. They plan events. They take selfies and love social media. They are social addicts!

These children are so attuned to their social world that sometimes you get the feeling that an idea left unexpressed would be a thought wasted. Social Secretaries often find it difficult to reflect and think, finding it easier to talk through issues and ideas.

The upside of having a Social Secretary is that they are often very dynamic, people persons who often do well in retail, marketing, events management and public relations and business. They are usually popular, outgoing, sensitive extroverts.

Many of them are chatty. A thought left unexpressed is a thought wasted. For this reason social media sites such as Facebook can be incredibly compelling for these children. They will share their breakfast menu with

the world. As they are helpful people they will be drawn to help others in need, making the world of Facebook particularly alluring and dangerous.

If their social media friends are experiencing difficulties, the Social Secretaries will often share in the despair.

Suggesting that they self-regulate their use of social media sites is a complete and utter waste of time. You will at times need to say firmly to Social Secretaries, 'Switch that off and do the things you need to do.'

These kids can find themselves easily led by others, fearful of conflict and distracted by others at school.

Some Social Secretaries are skilful with words and get enchanted by the sound of their own voices to the extent that you may need to reinforce a common family rule: 'Say excuse me if you have to interrupt.' Also they can be in such a rush to communicate that they will speak to you when they are in another room. To discourage conversations that are yelled between rooms in your home, feign deafness.

How you can help Social Secretaries

Social Secretaries are the group least likely to embark on a solo sailing trip around the world. They thrive on the presence of others. Unlocking the genius of Social Secretaries requires you to give them sufficient time with other people to enjoy life as well as some time for solo reflection to learn that they can think independently.

In terms of developing concentration skills, Social Secretaries often respond well to learning magic tricks, circus skills, acting and drama, singing and being a part of choirs, musical instruments, team sports that are not intensely competitive, puppetry and being given some responsibility for organising family functions.

A common issue for Social Secretaries (as well as others) is homework. The Social Secretaries and the Star Trekkers are especially prone to looking blankly at homework diaries. Both need to be helped to develop a system of writing down any homework that is set. You may need to set up a system of checking what homework is required with teachers.

To help develop these skills, find out from the teacher what homework is required. Then ask your child to write out what is required. Check whether your child has written it down correctly. Keep doing this until your Social Secretary has the skills of comprehending what is required.

You can also ask your kids to tell you everything they already know about the topic to be learned (this may not be much). Social Secretaries often find speaking easier than writing so asking them to tell you their ideas will probably be more productive than asking them to write down what they know.

It can be helpful for you to write down and map out the key points as they tell them to you. Then ask them to tell you the questions that they have and the parts they are uncertain about. Write these down as well. Use these questions to help them structure the format and content of their project or assignment. Consider which questions they can answer, those for which they'll need an explanation from you, those that need research, and what skills they need.

Wherever possible, relate abstract concepts to people, tribes or creatures. In mathematics turn formulas into sentences with words rather than symbols and ask children to explain their reasoning to you.

Some Social Secretaries need to learn how to enjoy their own company. Relying on others to entertain them all the time can leave them with no time to reflect or plan.

Help them to see the difference between being alone and loneliness. Parents can call time alone 'pause time', 'catch-up time' or 'thinking time'. Art projects are often a good way of starting this. Caring for pets is also helpful. Reading novels is another way for Social Secretaries to be involved with characters rather than relying on the people around them.

The Amplifiers

Last but certainly not least, we have the Amplifiers. The genius of Amplifiers is that they have drive in abundance and energy to burn. When they're really engaged in a challenge they have the determination and willpower to overcome major obstacles. These kids have an inbuilt ability to turn up the volume on whatever is happening around them.

Life for an Amplifier can be a series of adventures that they glide through with a devil-may-care look in their eyes. They are often energetic, brave and courageous people who seek out intense experiences in their lives. Unless they learn to moderate their volume controls, success at school is difficult. When tuned into the needs of others they are fantastic and inspirational leaders, teachers, managers and self-employed tradespeople.

You may need to explain to these children the type of behaviour that is expected in various settings. We all have to learn to behave differently in different settings. Amplifiers are often so busy making a racket they don't notice the context has changed.

Some of these children can grow into adults who you feel could take the world on but whenever they get a great idea, there's always an even greater one around the corner and they find it difficult to follow through.

Often these kids have very distinct patterns of concentration. At some times of the day they can be very focused. At other times, they are all over the place. You need to observe your child's rhythms very carefully and to shape learning times for reading and homework accordingly.

Amplifiers are very sensitive to heightened emotions. If there is conflict around they will pick up on it and often increase it. This means it is very important for you to consciously build and develop goodwill in your families. It may also be necessary to reduce or actively discourage competitiveness between family members.

How you can help Amplifiers

Unlock Amplifiers' genius by helping them select challenges that are worthy of them and by teaching them to modulate their volume. As Amplifiers like intensity, they will respond well to time trials, challenges and games that involve speed and action. Look carefully for activities that absorb and captivate them and try to diversify them.

These children need times to rev up and be very active followed by times when they can calm down or rest, so alternating times of activity with times of passive learning is helpful.

Some Amplifiers are so fast they focus only on the end point of a task. Helping them identify and plan the steps involved in achieving an outcome can be worthwhile. Helpful ways to guide Amplifiers include: 'If we want to do x, what are we going to need to do to get there? What do we do first, second, last?' Helping them identify the steps toward an outcome will improve their planning skills.

Most team games and sports involve times of being active alternating with times of being the audience to someone else's performance. The Amplifiers may need to be helped to see how times of non-active involvement can be used to think, plan and form strategies, otherwise their concentration drifts off.

Amplifiers usually have willpower in abundance. This is great, but it can also lead them to mistakenly think they can rely only on themselves. Not everyone has the same level of determination and energy as an Amplifier. Parents can help Amplifiers to realise that success is not just a matter of solo glory. There are times when you get much further by utilising and leveraging the skills of others. Some useful strategies include:

- personal best and positive coaching methods
- cooperative games
- team games.

My child is all or none of the above!

If you think your child is part Happy Wanderer, a flash of a Frequent Flyer, a touch of a Spy, a smidge of a Fidgeter as well as a being a bit of a Star Trekker, don't despair. Initially many children appear to be a bit of everything.

Parents often report that it takes a bit of time to really learn a child's concentration style. Take notice of when they seem to concentrate best and build on this.

Be prepared to experiment for a while before deciding the main features of your child's concentration pattern. It's worth taking the time to determine your child's pattern so that you can lead him or her towards success. Success involves determining the things you are good at – and doing more of them – while also having some awareness of the things you are not so great at, and not being overly bothered by them.

Schools generally try to make children good at everything. They usually have a curriculum or syllabus to teach. But this is not the way genius works. Geniuses find the things that they are good at and focus on them with great intensity while allowing other skills to become irrelevant.

Of course you don't want to narrow down children's skills too early, but knowing their concentration pattern and strengths will help you help them. When your child is struggling with something or finding it hard to comprehend, offering him or her alternatives can help: 'Well, why don't you make a drawing of it / record the steps on a recording device / turn it into a challenge / find a study group to work with / make a clay model of it?' Parents can encourage their children to utilise their strengths and learn in ways that suit them.

Playing to your strengths is important because in life, success is contagious. Get a whiff of success and you tend to go in search of getting more of it.

Don't be too concerned if you cannot see your child in the styles I have presented. These simply reflect children I've encountered during many years of clinical practice. I haven't described the entire world of people in this chapter. But keep looking for the things that your child naturally seems to concentrate on so you can help them to focus and flourish.

Developing concentration

Ages 2–4	■ Play concentration games such as Look at me and Silent statues. ■ Practise balancing, drawing and playing for extended periods. ■ Attach mobiles to ceilings with pictures of important groupings. ■ Play Repeat after me. ■ Dancing ■ Play hide and seek or tic-tac-toe. ■ Play with Matchbox cars, marbles, puppets, dolls, teddy bears. ■ Throwing, catching Nerf balls. ■ Immerse them in language. ■ Read aloud to them. ■ Sing songs like 'The Alphabet Song' and 'Old MacDonald Had a Farm'. ■ Read and re-read picture books. ■ Count fingers, toes, ears, eyes, noses, people. ■ Explore rock pools.
Ages 5–7	■ Play simple card games such as Snap and Fish. ■ Provide jigsaw puzzles to help motor skills, abstract reasoning and spatial organisation. ■ Play I-spy to develop language and attention. ■ Sit kids down to do collages, flow charts and posters to assist planning and organising information. ■ Provide coloured pieces of paper for kids to write on to assist memory.

	<ul><li>Use signs and reminders such as 'Pack Your Lunch!'</li><li>Display photos to remind them of past successes.</li><li>Use glitter pens, paints and crayons to make note-making exciting.</li><li>Play the card game Concentration to strengthen memory skills.</li><li>Play 'Simon says'.</li><li>Dance, roller skate, make sandcastles.</li><li>Play with remote control cars, train sets, telescopes, mosaics, Power Rangers, model cars.</li><li>Practise simple model building – aeroplanes, figures, robots.</li><li>Play Monopoly (Junior), Chinese chequers.</li><li>Be a spy, birdwatch.</li></ul>
Ages 8–11	<ul><li>Play Twister or musical chairs.</li><li>Play handball to improve visual motor skills (eye–hand coordination) and team skills (especially for doubles).</li><li>Build kites and fly them.</li><li>Play with Lego to improve gross and fine motor coordination.</li><li>Do mazes to practise problem-solving.</li><li>Learn gymnastics and dance.</li><li>Go to pony clubs.</li><li>Learn musical instruments like violin, guitar, piano, cello and trumpet.</li><li>Build models to assist fine motor skills.</li><li>Play with blocks, dice and tiles to learn mathematics.</li><li>Have some periods of learning in silence.</li><li>Use soft gentle music to lower their levels of energy.</li></ul>

	<ul><li>Encourage rhyming games and reading and writing poetry.</li><li>Listen to recorded stories and audio books.</li><li>Play Pictionary, Monopoly, jigsaw puzzles or games with dice with the whole family.</li><li>Dance, jump rope, throw a frisbee, play with a hula hoop or yo-yo.</li><li>Try pottery, sculpture, more intricate model building.</li><li>Practise magic tricks.</li></ul>
Ages 12–18	<ul><li>Play Battleships to learn about sequencing.</li><li>Play chess to encourage problem-solving and strategic thinking.</li><li>Play Chinese chequers to practise planning.</li><li>Play Risk, backgammon, card games or dominoes.</li><li>Learn and play musical instruments.</li><li>Join a band or choir.</li><li>Do theatre sports.</li><li>Practise poetry slam-dunks (poems that are created on the run with each person adding a word – good for listening, focusing and improvisational thinking).</li><li>Make a video or podcasts.</li><li>Play computer games or alternate reality gaming.</li><li>Go geo-caching.</li><li>Practise meditation and mindfulness.</li><li>Dance.</li><li>Go skating or go-karting.</li><li>Try clay modelling.</li><li>Experiment with fashion design.</li></ul>

CHAPTER 5

Encouraging effective thinking

A problem is an opportunity in drag.

Paul Hawken

A man in London walked into the produce section of his local supermarket and asked to buy half a head of lettuce. The boy working in the department told him that they only sold whole heads of lettuce. The man was insistent that the boy ask the manager about the matter.

Walking into the back room, the boy said to the manager, 'Some old grump wants to buy a half a head of lettuce.'

As he finished his sentence, he turned around to find that the man was standing right behind him, so he quickly added, 'And this gentleman kindly offered to buy the other half.'

The manager approved the deal and the man went on his way. Later, the manager said to the boy, 'I was impressed with the way you got yourself out of that situation earlier. We like people who can think on their feet here. Where are you from, son?'

'New Zealand, sir,' the boy replied.

'Why did you leave New Zealand?' the manager asked.

The boy said, 'Sir, there's nothing but prostitutes and rugby players there.'

'Is that right?' replied the manager. 'My wife is from New Zealand!'

'Really?' replied the boy, 'Who'd she play for?'

This is a lovely example of quick thinking that was circulating as an email recently. (I've cleaned it up a bit.)

From the moment they are born, children are conducting an experiment into how life works. Alison Gopnik describes them as the scientist in the crib. They form hypotheses, test them and run trials to determine their effectiveness. For example:

- If I yell loudly will my parents come to me?
- If I add tears what will that do?
- If I say I can't sleep will I get to stay up?
- If I throw something at my brother do I get attention?
- If I don't try at school do I get to leave and retire early?
- If I throw a party while my parents are out of town will they find out?

Parents are the guinea pigs in their children's laboratories. To rise above that status you, as a parent, need to help them shift their focus from conducting investigations into what makes you tick to what makes the world work.

As they get older little kids are like roosters; up at dawn and into everything. They are inquisitive. They ask lots of questions. Why does the moon shine at night? Why doesn't it shine during the day? Where does the light go when you turn it off? Why is the sky blue? Why is water wet? Why are dogs hairy?

Kids think at a million miles an hour. They are like sponges drinking in and absorbing information. The big question is not how to make kids curious. They are already itching to learn. The question is how to keep them curious.

Unfortunately, by about six or seven years of age, too many kids lose their desire to learn. They stop asking questions. They start worrying about knowing the right answer. Some resentfully become aware they are not at the top of the class and perceive themselves as failures. Of course this doesn't happen for all kids but for far too many, the lights are dimmed down.

The real issue for parents is not how to get kids thinking but how to keep them thinking; how to keep the spark of enquiry bright rather than being dampened down to a dull glow.

The basis of success in life is thinking. Improving at anything requires *effective thinking*. The good news is that once you can think more effectively, you can apply these skills to all areas of life.

Effective thinking methods and tools can be described, taught and learned. I outline them in the next sections to give you some ideas about how you can expand thinking and keep curiosity alive. In a complex world it is those who can think clearly, deeply and simply who will stand out. Your role as a parent is to help your child to develop very simple ideas first. Clear the clutter and expose what is really important then see what's missing.

Helping your child to think clearly is a long-term project. I doubt that you will use all these thinking methods at the one time. Hopefully, you will find ways to use each of them over the years. Clarity of thought not only leads to inventiveness and creativity, it also creates happy lives.

Same, same but different

The Thai people have a saying that encapsulates all of human thought: 'Same, same but different'. The way people form concepts in their heads is through analogy and difference.

People think in patterns. These patterns or schema are formed when we work out how two things are similar and then differentiate them from a third thing.

As the world becomes saturated with knowledge based on internet searches, people have access to lots of teeny bits of information. However, being able to access information is not the same as knowing it, and knowing it is not the same as understanding how to apply it. Watching medical shows does not make you a surgeon. For this reason you need to build, support and extend the connections between pieces of information by asking your child to consider what different things have in common.

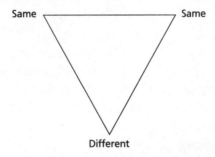

In the Western world, same, same but different thinking is known as the identification of similarities and differences and results in a massive 45 percentile improvement in academic results. (3) That takes children from a situation where they are performing better than 50 per cent of their class to performing better than 95 per cent of the class.

People form concepts naturally, but you can encourage this in your child by asking questions like:

- How are an apple and an orange alike?
- How are a dog and a giraffe alike? How are both different from a buffalo?
- How are gothic architecture and Art Nouveau alike?
- How was the American War of Independence similar to the French Revolution?
- How are the speed of light and the speed of sound alike? How are they different?

Know and understand simple ideas

I begin with an idea and then it becomes something else.

Pablo Picasso

Most acts of genius come from very simple ideas combined in new ways to create a whole new way of looking at things. Albert Einstein once said that imagination is more important than knowledge and he was right, but you have to have the knowledge first.

The best way for a child to acquire basic knowledge is in the company of a loving parent who is aware that part of their role is to help their kids explore and understand the world. Parenting is a learning opportunity. Parents are looked to for answers to the most bizarre questions. One of the most powerful ways of encouraging genius in kids is to say, 'Well, I don't know the answer to that but let's find out.'

Let's imagine a child asks you where the wind comes from. You could just give him or her a brief answer (eg the ocean) or use a search engine to get a broader answer. But this is an opportunity to turn the question into a powerful learning opportunity. Of course, no parent has the time to do this with every question that children pose, but there will be occasions when you are able to take a question and use it to link a range of issues.

In terms of answering where the wind comes from, you could do this by getting a world weather map and identifying the places where the forecast is for wind and where it is calm. You could then get a weather chart showing high and low systems and work out which way the wind is blowing in different regions.

If there are cyclones or hurricanes you could learn about those as well. If your child shows an interest you could then shift onwards to the topics of lightning and clouds and rain. You could then go outdoors and fly a kite or take them surfing or sailing.

Stretching ideas is an important skill but don't overdo it. If you see their eyes starting to glaze over, either ask them if there is anything else that interests them about wind or stop. Don't overcook the goose.

Start by ensuring your kids know and understand basic ideas and knowledge. Then build on this knowledge if they're interested. Their passions will likely change over time but use their interests to stretch ideas. Also use the opportunity to demonstrate that even adults learn new things. For example, you might say, 'Do you remember asking me where the wind comes from last week? Well, I learned something new about that ...' As Dr. Seuss put it, 'Oh, the places you can go!'

Use facts as bridges to understanding

Instead of just focusing on facts, put your parenting energies into helping your child see how the facts they learn link together. This converts information into understanding. Having an encyclopaedic knowledge of the history of the royal lineage of Britain may not be essential in a world where we can simply look up such things on the internet. In our world, many facts are easily accessible; but thinking, judgement and wisdom are scarce.

Some facts are important foundation skills but facts on any topic are only the skeleton of knowledge. The body is built by combining facts with learning.

Traditional schooling divides learning into discrete boxes known as subjects. Yet we know that genius works by bridging the barriers between areas of knowledge, not by dividing it up. History, for example, is taught as a series of disconnected events – Greek history, Roman history, Chinese history – often without providing the links between them. A better model is proposed by Susan Wise Bauer, author of *The Well-Trained Mind*, who suggests creating with children timelines for all world events that have occurred in an historical period. She suggests having a long piece of paper in the hallway divided into time zones and marking key events. Help children find the location on a map or even better a globe.

Use facts to lead your child to more interesting questions. For example, if we think about the classification of animals, mammals can be defined as being warm blooded, give birth to live young (rather than eggs) and have hair over most of their body.

You can then guide children to think further: Are kittens, dogs and koalas mammals? (Yes.) Are snakes and crocodiles? (No, they lay eggs.) Are most fish mammals? (No, they don't have hair.) Could there be mammals that live in the sea or rivers? (Yes, whales and otters.) Are there any mammals that lay eggs? (Yes, the echidna.)

Up until the age of four years you will be guiding your child's learning. Partly you will do this by carrying on a running commentary of many of the things that you do with them.

After four or five years of age, you will progressively become more explorative as you extend your child's knowledge. It is the thinking that happens when we use facts and apply them that allows genius to flourish.

We do need children to learn some facts. Obviously it is hard to analyse the meaning of an essay if you are stumbling over the use of grammatical rules, or understand complete advanced mathematical equations without knowing multiplication tables.

Bring reading into your family life by asking children, 'Can you pass the salt, please? It has an S on it.' Have a set time each day for reading. Many children are ready to read before they are ready to write.

Bring numbers into everyday family life. Children need to learn their multiplication tables and associated divisions. You can assist in this by asking your child to find four apples. Then ask, 'If I cut them in half how many pieces will I have? How about if I cut them into fourths?'

Card games like Uno and Fish all help develop children's number sense. Count fingers and toes. Play hide and seek by counting to ten, then for a twist, count by twos, fives or tens before calling out, 'Coming ready or not!'

Children don't naturally form thinking bridges that link ideas but you can show them how to think by raising questions, and showing the links and connections. For example, you can teach children the two times table and then use it when sorting the laundry: 'Dad has ten socks, how many pairs is that?' Or 'I have ten cakes and five children. How many cakes can each child have if I share them out fairly?'

Ask children, 'Can you tell me all the things you know about 8?' Children can write or draw things like:

$4 + 4 = 8$

$6 + 2 = 8$

$5 + 3 = 8$

$4 \times 2 = 8$

$10 - 2 = 8$

$3 \times 8 = 24$

$24 \div 3 = 8$

8 is the number of hours most people sleep

The 8th month of the year is August

8 is an even number

8 is how old I am

Granddad is 80

$80 = 8 \times 10$, so my Granddad is ten times older than I am

8 is $2 \times 2 \times 2$ or 2^3

An octopus has 8 tentacles

An octagon has 8 sides

Rowing boats at the races are called eights

Helping children to see and think through these links expands their thinking and allows their genius to flourish. It also encourages the flexibility of thinking. The answer might be '8', but how many questions could we ask to get there?

Soak it up! The fine art of observation

The way to get good ideas is to get lots of ideas and throw the bad ones away.

Linus Pauling

Another way of helping your child to be an effective thinker is to sharpen their powers of observation.

Babies are excellent at observing people. Keeping that childlike open-mindedness into adulthood is tricky. In a world that seems to suffer from attention deficiencies, people who are aware, mindful and observant stand out.

The art of noticing and observing is not as simple as it might seem. It's not just the passive process of letting objects enter into your visual field; it's about knowing what and how to observe.

To be a sharp observer means thinking about and making sense of the things we see, hear, feel, touch and smell. It is about richly immersing yourself in all of your senses and then asking yourself, 'What can I learn from this?'

Observation kicks the whole genius mind into gear. Geniuses are able to hang on to the natural curiosity of their childhood and apply it with laser-like ferocity to areas they are interested in.

Something truly dreadful happens to lots of kids when their sparky interest in learning is converted into a passive process of receiving information. As a society, we are doing something very odd with learning. We take it out of the realm of adventure and fun and start to think of it as hard work. We segment learning into little bits of knowledge that schools call 'lessons'. Learning then moves from something we naturally do to something we 'have to do'.

Most kids are naturally astute so their skills can always be developed. Parents who can sharpen their children's skills of observation help unlock their genius. The types of activities that do this include:

- people spotting
- detective games
- mystery films
- spot the difference
- picking what is missing in drawings
- memory games such as ten objects on a tray
- guessing who objects in a bag belong to
- interpreting photos and artworks
- solving puzzles and mysteries.

One good activity is called 'The feeling detectives'. This is a fun way parents and kids can pick up clues about people they see. Ask kids to guess what sort of day a person passing on the street has had, what mood they are in, what they might be doing, what sort of job they do and so on. This not only builds observational skills but also builds emotional intelligence.

Older kids and teenagers may look at you with a wary eye when you start this activity but assure them it is helpful romantically. It will help them pick the right person.

Observation is not just about seeing what is there; it is also about seeing what is not there. When Disney World was opened after Walt Disney passed away, someone commented what a shame it was that Walt didn't live to see it. One of Disney's friends replied, 'It's because Walt could see it that it is here.'

In 1937 a grocer named Sylvan Goldman realised that a person could only buy what they could carry with their two hands. By thinking about what was not there, Mr Goldman took some wooden folding chairs, attached wheels and a basket and invented the shopping trolley.

Observation is about the senses, particularly seeing. What raises it to the level of genius is being able to think about how things link together and at times, what is missing.

Don't be content with initial impressions. Many people make a first observation, use it to make a judgement and then stop thinking. Rex remains comfortable and tells Albert to stop working. Geniuses are insatiably curious. They not only notice, they keep noticing. As their observations build they continue to ask questions of themselves to check if their initial observations are correct or incorrect.

This is the great lesson of Little Red Riding Hood. Not everything that sits up in a bed and calls itself a grandmother is actually a grandmother. It is important to keep observing.

Make mistakes

Ever tried. Ever failed. No matter. Try again. Fail again.
Fail better.

Samuel Beckett

The ability to make mistakes is essential for genius. You simply can't get many things right until you know how to get them wrong. Encourage your children to see mistakes as a step closer to getting something right.

Some of the best discoveries came from mistakes. Christopher Columbus was searching for India when he landed in America. Alexander Fleming discovered penicillin when he noticed that one of his petri dishes developed a mould that was resistant to bacteria. People who don't make mistakes don't make anything.

Creating something new involves making a lot of mistakes. One example is the bestselling Dyson vacuum cleaner. The inventor made 5,127 prototypes of the vacuum before getting it right. 'There were 5,126 failures. But I learned from each one. That's how I came up with a solution. So I don't mind failure.'

In Paris, there is a festival of errors to give children experience in making mistakes and to challenge intellectual timidity.

On 25 May 1961, John F. Kennedy challenged that by the end of that decade a person would have been to the moon and safely back again. The National Space Council started work on the mission the next day, but they didn't suit up an astronaut straightaway. Three years later NASA smashed Ranger 7 into the moon at a velocity of 5,862 miles per hour. It took fifteen trials before the successful and gentle moon landing of Apollo 11 on 16 July 1969.

You have to get it wrong in order to get it right. If you are stuck, a mistake can be just the thing to unstick you. Any creative achievement is the result of a series of missteps. Failures can clarify the pathway towards success. In the 1970s three guys invented a way of analysing traffic called Traf-O-Data. It failed miserably. But they learned from their failure and started another company. The next one they called Microsoft.

People don't get a chance to be great before they've had a chance to be not so great. Post-It Notes were developed when Spencer Silver at 3M research laboratories tried to make a strong adhesive but only managed to make a weak one instead. The Beatles slugged it out for years playing in clubs and bars before becoming famous.

Removing the anxiety about how to be immediately successful is what allows kids to play, explore, dream and be creative.

Encourage your children to make mistakes. Ask kids to offer an answer even if they know it is wrong. Then ask them why they think it is wrong. This encourages kids to opt in to a thinking process rather than having them shrug and look blank. Learning how to move from an incorrect answer towards a solution is the way most great thinkers succeed.

Build a family culture of being brave enough to make mistakes. Most of us cover up the gaps in our knowledge, hide our mistakes and hope that no-one ever finds out. The cost of this is that we stop being inquisitive.

When you build a family culture that allows for mistakes, start with yourself. Allow yourself twelve small mistakes each day and when the first one happens think, 'One down, only eleven to go.'

> *I've missed more than 9000 shots in my career. I've lost almost 300 games. Twenty-six times I've been trusted to take the game winning shot ... and missed. I've failed over and over and over again in my life. That is why I succeed.*
>
> Michael Jordan

Question yourself

Asking questions is a sign of intelligence. Genius is seeing what everyone else sees and thinking what no-one else has thought.

Socrates is reported to have said that all thinking begins with wondering. He based his entire teaching method not on providing answers but on asking questions. You can't think clearly unless you are able to ask good questions. Questions require children to think.

Geniuses are not afraid to ask really basic questions. It is by asking the questions that others think are too stupid to ask, that they come up with brilliant ideas.

> *What everybody believes in is not what's actually true.*
>
> Galileo

Once geniuses feel comfortable asking the most obvious questions they can think of, they can then start to ask the strangest, weirdest, most out-there questions they can think of. This enables them to take those answers and ideas and link them in new and interesting ways.

Most geniuses rearrange ideas and connect them in original ways. Albert Einstein developed the theory of relativity by daydreaming about riding on a sunbeam. The physicist Niel Bohrs, when trying to understand quantum mechanics, would shift his position and his investigations on alternate days. One day he would assume quantum mechanics was a true description of our world and look at the implications, the next he would assume it was false.

Listen to a position that is different to your own. Teach your child to play 'devil's advocate' to their own ideas. One way to encourage children to question themselves is to use thinking cards that can prompt an inquiry. You can either make up sets of these yourself or obtain some from www.inyahead.com.au.

Some questions you can use to prompt your child include:

- Why is this issue important?
- How does x relate to y?
- What would be an example?
- What is an alternative?
- What do you think is true about x?
- How do you know?
- Why do you think that is true?
- Do you have any evidence for that?
- What other information do you need?
- Could you explain your reasons to me?
- Are these reasons adequate?
- How can you find out more?
- What are you sure about and what are you uncertain about?

Use thinking routines

Thinking routines are questions Ron Richhardt and his colleagues developed for teachers to use but they can also be used by parents to help children think. The following questions help children to dig deeper into a topic or area of learning.

See, think, wonder

You can use this to develop a sense of curiosity. Take a picture or painting and ask your child the following questions:

- What do you see?
- What do you think is going on?
- What does it make you wonder?

Zoom in

You could also show a small part of a picture and ask:

- What do you see or notice?
- What do you think is going on?

Keep revealing more of the image and repeat the question. This encourages hypothesising and using evidence.

Think, puzzle, explore

You can use this method to help your child to expand their thinking about an issue or a topic.

- What do you think you know about this?
- What questions do you have about this?
- What do you find puzzling? How might we explore these puzzles?

Headlines

Ask your child to write a headline that summarises the main point of a story or historical event.

- Dinosaur alert: asteroid hits earth!
- Baseball game goes round and round.
- *Titanic*: the unsinkable sinks

True? False? Maybe?

One game you can play with your child is true, false or maybe.

- Dogs can have fleas. Does my dog have fleas? (Maybe)
- All birds lay eggs. Do magpies lay eggs? (True)
- Sally is one year older than James. Is Sally taller than James? (Maybe)
- My little sister cries when I won't let her play with me. Does my little sister hate me? (False)
- Barry thinks Jane is good at drawing. Is Jane good at drawing? (Maybe)
- That is a safe way to go to school but it's very dangerous in foggy weather. Will it be safe tomorrow? (Maybe)
- Tyron would have played tennis last night if his friend had showed up. Did Tyron play tennis last night? (False)

In a world that often stops thinking, being able to play around with these types of ideas puts your child well ahead of the pack.

When in doubt, map it out

While many children have preferred ways of concentrating (see Chapter 4), it is best to start with a visual outline linking the ideas. Brain bubble maps, also called mind maps, connect ideas and help children see the links between concepts. As an example, have a look at the brain bubble map of the concept of 'thinking' below.

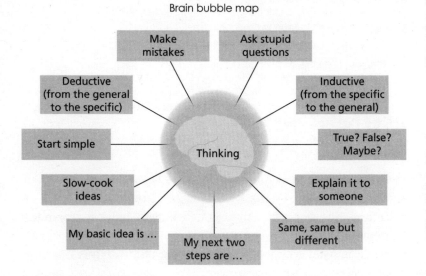

Brain bubble map

Slow-cook ideas

Our world seems intent on valuing the quickest answer rather than the best ideas. While the raconteur often comes up with the wittiest retort, the genius knows they need to slow-cook ideas.

Your inner Rex wants to stop thinking as soon as possible and get back to having a rest. As much as your brain wants to rush to a speedy answer, put the brakes on. The first answer is often the least creative one that most people would think of. Sleep on it, take a walk, do something else for a while or take a nap. Allow your brain to surprise you with the depth of its ingenuity.

You can help your child learn this by stopping a discussion from time to time and saying, 'Let's leave our thinking until tomorrow and see what ideas we have then.' *Teaching children how to sit with not knowing can be just as important as helping them find out an answer.*

Explain it to understand it

Nothing helps you learn something better than explaining or teaching it to someone else. Two of the best questions parents can ask are:

- Can you tell me about it?
- Wow, that's interesting. What makes you say that?

The job of parents is not to correct the explanation. Being told their painting of a purple duck is wrong because ducks aren't usually purple is not what kids need. Rather, the process of telling your ideas to someone who gives you total acceptance is mind expanding.

Many parents worry that if they don't correct ideas then their child will not learn properly. Replicating the critical feedback all too often given in schools makes kids cautious and gives them the impression that there is only one answer. This is not the pathway towards genius.

Now obviously this has its limits. The word 'apple' does begin with the letter 'A' and 1 + 1 does equal 2 and it can be worth pointing this out. For more intricate thoughts, helping children to derive their own understanding through acceptance and gentle clarifying of questions is best.

Make thinking fun

Don't spend your days in a daze. Learning should be play. Twisting, distorting, stretching ideas can be great fun. Turn them upside down, inside out, stretch them forwards and back. Play with them. Help kids to realise that ideas can handle a bit of rough play and that answers should be treated with disrespect and questioned, if not interrogated.

Creativity often arises when we treat existing ideas with a playful disdain. Comedy routines beautifully illustrate this. Abbot and Costello's classic 'Who's on first?' sketch hilariously plays with the meaning of words. The Two Ronnies (Ronnie Barker and Ronnie Corbett) were masters of this art. Of course, we can also try to give children a taste for Monty Python, *The Goon Show* and other absurd comedies.

Take the Philosopher's Path

Near Kyoto in Japan there is a path that people walk called the Philosopher's Path. Nishida Kitaro, one of Japan's most famous philosophers, thought and meditated while walking this route on his daily commute to Kyoto University. Following a canal lined with cherry trees, people now use this path to think.

For thousands of years, people have used labyrinths or circles of contemplation to walk as they reflect and think. Having a family ritual where you walk somewhere safe and pleasant while thinking may be worth practising.

Deductive and inductive thinking

This last thinking method is the most complex so don't be dismayed if it takes you a bit of time to get your head around it. For the readers who are advanced philosophers, I apologise in advance. My simplification of very complex ideas so that most children and parents can use them may send shivers up your spine and cause you to cringe intellectually.

People don't get ideas, they make them. For children to move beyond just being the recipient of other people's ideas, they need to learn to think. There are two different ways we can think our way through things.

Deductive thinking is where we make a conclusion based on a set of ideas that we have tested and linked together. Science experiments and detective work are two examples. Sherlock Holmes's detective-type reasoning involves taking a series of clues and putting them together in the most logical way to explain the circumstances.

Inductive thinking is when we make a series of observations and come to a broader theory about how the world works. Sociologists, for example, take a specific observation and try to make a general theory about human behaviour.

Both the detective (using deductive reasoning) and the sociologist (using inductive reasoning) are applying knowledge to fit another situation. Thinking is combining information in new ways.

In reality we use both of these types of thinking a lot of the time, but it is useful for kids to be aware that you can consciously use different approaches to think through the same idea.

Below is a summary of the key differences between deductive and inductive thinking.

The processes of thinking	
Deductive	**Inductive**
Deductive thinking moves from a general idea to a specific example.	Inductive thinking works from a specific example or idea to a general concept or theory.
One way of remembering this is to recall that 'deduce' rhymes with 'reduce'.	One way to remember this is to recall that inductive begins with 'I' and is about increasing.
To deduce is to reduce from lots of ideas to a main idea or theory – from the general to a specific answer.	To think inductively is to increase the applicability of an idea – from a specific observation to a general idea or theory.

Often used to understand events that have happened in the past.	Often used to make predictions about the future.
Comes to a conclusion.	Comes to a premise or theory.
Narrow and tests an idea.	Exploratory and open.
Starts with truths that lead you to see what else will be true if that idea is true.	Starts with an observation that determines what general conclusions could be made from that information.

An example of deductive and inductive thinking	
Deductive	**Inductive**
Happy cats purr.	All cats purr when they are happy.
My cat purrs when I pat her ears.	When I pat my cat's ears she purrs.
My cat likes it when I pat her ears.	If I want my cat to be happy I should pat her ears more often.

I suspect my example of cat's moods and purring may not seem very earth shattering to you. Both types of thinking have their strengths and their weaknesses.

Deductive thinking is great for linking ideas to produce a testable theory. But! We need to test the theory out rather than just making our ideas fit the situation.

Inductive thinking is great for turning our observations into a theory of how things work. But! If our observations are incomplete, they can mislead us and sometimes lead us to make judgements that are unwarranted. Racial prejudices, for example, are based on faulty inductive thinking.

Deductive and inductive thinking can lead us to different conclusions	
Deductive	**Inductive**
Successful students do homework.	Children complain about homework.
I want my child to be successful.	Unhappy children resent school.
I need to find a way to get my child to do homework.	Schools should not make students do homework.

Whichever of these positions you find most compelling, it is useful to be able to weigh up issues, consider how we make conclusions and understand the limitations of our thinking.

Asking the right questions

A great example of the need to ask good questions and then question the answers you get was made in the *Pink Panther* movies with the character Inspector Clouseau. Inspector Clouseau enters a hotel where a dog is sitting in the foyer so he asks the desk clerk, 'Does your dog bite?'

The desk clerk replies, 'No, my dog does not bite.'

Clouseau pats the dog and the dog tries to bite him.

Clouseau indignantly says to the desk clerk, 'I thought you said your dog does not bite.'

The desk clerk replies, 'That is not my dog.'

Before you get all huffy and think that inductive thinking is just noticing things and applying them willy-nilly to the rest of the world, you need to know that deductive thinking is also not perfect. This was superbly illustrated by Douglas Adams in his series of books *The Hitchhiker's Guide to the Galaxy*. It showed how René Descartes's axiom 'I think therefore I am' can mislead us, by using an example of a whale contemplating its own existence.

Here is a summary of the whale's deductive thinking.

> *I think therefore I am*
> *I have been living on krill*
> *Krill do not think*
> *Therefore krill do not exist*
> *I have been living on nothing.*
> *No wonder I'm starving.*

We all use deductive and inductive reasoning all the time. Learning to play with them and know their limitations is helpful.

Many people start to struggle with mathematics when it shifts away from inductive thinking.

If I have one apple and one orange how many pieces of fruit do I have? Of course it's two. The general principle of $1 + 1 = 2$ applies. That's inductive thinking. But when a question doesn't have an observable answer, deductive thinking is required.

For equations such as $x + 3 = 6$, $x \times 9 = 27$ and $x - 3 = 0$, finding x requires you to deduce that the answer is three from a number of examples.

Many people stop thinking because they prefer certainty to uncertainty – even if that uncertainty is wrong.

Geniuses are people who keep thinking, keep asking questions and keep wondering. They learn that playing with ideas is fun and that there is often more than one answer.

Inductive thinking is imaginative and requires awareness as well as the capacity to think about how something you observe might apply in other situations.

Deductive thinking requires observation and then putting ideas together to produce a testable idea.

Ways to help your child become an effective thinker	
Ages 2–4	▪ Help your child to see simple associations. ▪ Ensure familiarity with basic ideas such as sunrise, sunset, weather, seasons and how they change, how animals can be similar and how they can be different. ▪ Move from playing with one object such as a rattle to seeing what happens when you combine two objects such as a rattle and a drum. ▪ Encourge alphabet puzzles, simple jigsaws, sand play and making mud cakes. ▪ Language is the building block of thought – talk about comparing and contrasting, find similarities and differences between things and discuss them.
Ages 5–7	▪ Start conversation topics and link them to other topics. ▪ Play spot the difference games. ▪ Do puzzles and read puzzle books. ▪ Play simple memory games. ▪ Talk about why making mistakes is important. ▪ Talk about how things can change – clouds change shape, the tides change, the moon looks different at different times of the month, water can turn into ice and can be boiled to make a cup of tea.

	<ul><li>Encourage join the dots games and Lego.</li><li>Make a model of the solar system using oranges, basketballs etc.</li><li>Conduct investigations into topics in which your child is interested.</li><li>Help your child to do basic research – internet, encyclopaedias, YouTube clips, TED talks.</li><li>Analyse stories that you read. Ask questions like:<ul><li>What was the main point or message of the story?</li><li>Who was the hero?</li><li>Was there a bad person or villain? Who?</li><li>What was your favourite bit?</li><li>Who did you like most/least? Why?</li></ul></li><li>Explore basic forces – gravity, astronomy, speed, time, magnetic fields, light.</li><li>Play with magnets and mirrors.</li><li>Build model space ships.</li><li>Set goals for the week with them.</li></ul>
Ages 8–11	<ul><li>Talk about practising detective-like reasoning. Follow clues. This is the basis of deductive reasoning.</li><li>Use facts as bridges to broaden understanding. Link several ideas together to form a theory about how the world works. Test out the theory. This is the basis of inductive reasoning.</li><li>You might also wish to use thinking tools such as Edward de Bono's thinking hats and PMI (pluses, minuses, interesting).</li><li>Investigate great ideas and great thinkers.</li><li>Use clues to come up with answers.</li></ul>

	■ Use answers to come up with general theories. ■ Draw out complex ideas such as the idea that many things have advantages and disadvantages or pros and cons. ■ Do puzzles. ■ Play Cluedo, 20 Questions, Celebrity Heads. ■ Visit a planetarium. ■ Visit or access natural history museums. ■ Help your child to conduct more detailed research investigations into areas of interest – forming basic questions, making informed guesses or hypotheses, conducting investigations or experiments and making conclusions. ■ Play charades. ■ Read detective and spy novels. ■ Watch comedy shows that play with the meaning of words. ■ Teach the PICCA method (see Chapter 6).
Ages 12-18	■ Discuss the ideas of deductive and inductive reasoning. The terms will be new, but hopefully both will have been used between the ages of 8 and 11. ■ Help to make it visual by using mind maps, bubble maps, planners. ■ Teach your child to debate ideas and look at pros and cons. ■ Read and watch mystery and horror books and films where things are not always as they initially seem. ■ Read detective and spy stories. ■ Discuss probability. Use dice rolls to explore this concept.

- Philosophical debates and discussions are wonderful ways of expanding teenagers' minds. Find controversial issues or questions and discuss them with them such as:
  - If we put injured animals out of their misery, why shouldn't we do the same for humans?
  - If we eat cows and sheep, why don't we eat cats and dogs?
  - If carbon emissions are polluting the planet, why shouldn't we ban cars?
- As teenagers often have great ideals, find an area that they are passionate about and investigate it. Have them write a letter to the editor of a newspaper and a letter to a politician. Talk about how thinking can lead to actions that change the world.
- Keep a journal of ideas.
- Play around with brain and logic puzzles.

CHAPTER 6

Teaching kids to plan

Success doesn't come to us, we go to it.

Mawa Collins

When Walter Mischel offered young children the choice between eating one marshmallow straightaway or two when he returned (provided they didn't eat the first while he was out of the room for 15 minutes), he really started something. Only 30 per cent of the children in his study were able to resist the temptation of the first marshmallow.

The ability to not take the marshmallow and stuff it into your mouth was equated with self-control. The ability to resist doing the first thing that comes into your mind turned out to be a powerful predictor of success in life. The children who were able to resist the temptation of the first marshmallow and hold off to get the second were 30 years later more likely to have succeeded in school and careers, were healthier, made better choices and kept their relationships intact. Who would have thought resisting a marshmallow could be so powerful?

David Fergusson studied over 1200 children from Christchurch, New Zealand, up to their thirtieth birthday, and found that their ability to control their first impulses predicted better functioning in life and lower criminal involvement.

Much of your child's happiness will be determined by their ability to make positive plans and then make decisions and follow through on them. Teach children to ask themselves, 'If I do this, then what?' The ability to plan is really a victory of Albert over Rex. Rex wants to do the first thing and stay as comfortable as possible. Albert plans and weighs up the rewards as well as the consequences.

If we translate the marshmallow results into another context we find that the ability to resist playing a computer game before completing the study needed for a project is highly predictive of success in life.

Geniuses do the hard stuff first. They know that if they allow themselves to goof off and laze about they'll never get to do the things that really matter. It is a rare child, however, who comes with in-built impulse controls. Most children have a rampant Rex who lurches around wanting this then wanting that.

The world also seems to promote a sense of frantic immediate gratification. I want it now! Many people suffer from FONK and FOMO.

FONK stands for 'fear of not knowing'; FOMO for 'fear of missing out'. This leads children to be saturated with information but impoverished with wisdom. They are so connected to social media and computer-based stimulation they have no time to reflect, think and plan.

In a world that emphasises the immediate gratification of our impulsive Rex, it is the people who can choose to delay and give their Albert a chance to plan who become geniuses.

Enough reading. Let's do some planning. Have a go at completing the maze below.

Brain maze

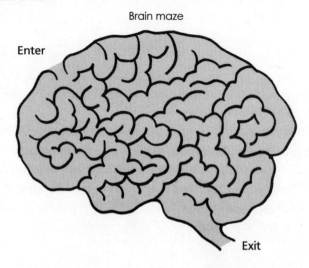

How did you go about it? My guess is you had to look ahead and consider your options before working out the steps to take.

This process requires you to consider and reconsider. To act or not to act. Just as successful tennis, baseball and cricket players need to know when to hit the ball and when to not hit the ball, we all need to learn how to consider and reconsider.

Teaching children to create planning trails

Charts, sticky notes and erasable whiteboards are useful things to have, though you can just scratch a planning trail in the mud if you want to.

I'll use the example of using sticky notes. Ask children to write out or draw the outcome or result they want on one note. Then have them write each possible small step towards achieving that outcome on different sticky notes. You can use different coloured ones if that helps them.

Move these around into a sequence that seems logical. It's a bit like constructing a trail to a destination.

Planning trail

Prompt children by asking questions like:

- What do you want the end result to be?
- Why do you want that result? (Asking children to explain their thoughts will often clarify if the outcome they have expressed is really the outcome they want.)

- What do you think might be the first thing we could do to get closer to that result? (Younger children may leap to a stage that is just before the result. If so, help them to find the intervening steps by saying, 'That's great. What do you think needs to happen between the starting point and this step?')
- What do you think might happen next?
- What do we need to do next?

Give them time to think. Be supportive but try not to rush in with helpful suggestions. (If there is any chance of them contributing to your wellbeing in your more senior years, they need to learn how to plan.)

Sometimes there are a couple of alternative ways of attaining the same outcome. In those cases help children make two more trails.

With complex or important plans, it can be useful to help children learn to place their planning trail somewhere safe and look at it several times over the next few days. Connections and ideas or options that were previously unconsidered often come when we reflect.

Planning trails may seem fairly simple but teaching them to your children will give them a skill and an advantage that lasts a lifetime. When completing exams, learning how to outline a plan for the answer before starting to write is extremely helpful. If they are to discover a new land, write a play or concerto, isolate a new chemical element, cure a major disease, paint a cathedral ceiling or weave a magnificent tapestry, children will need to plan.

Charts and maps

So far we have discussed planning in terms of actions taken towards achieving a result. Children also need to know how to plan ideas. It is also useful to know how to group, link and connect ideas and to sometimes think about what they know for certain, what they have some doubts about and what they don't know in order to plan how to progress in an area of learning. Planners, colour-coded charts, essay organisers and outlines all help children plan.

A good visual way to teach children to plan ideas is to help them create charts about an idea. For example, you might find a feather on a walk and stick it at the centre of a large piece of paper. They can then write the world 'feather'. Now ask them to draw what animal has feathers. Then they put the chart somewhere they can see it and whenever they find something related – a fact, a song, an actual thing – it goes on the chart too. Connecting ideas is a powerful way of organising thinking and builds planning and observational skills.

Charts can also be used to outline the frontiers of our knowledge. Ask children to draw a landscape chart like the one below.

Landscape chart

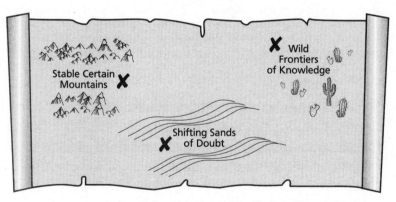

Have children place different pieces of information about a topic into these areas. Facts they are confident are true are put in the Stable Certain Mountains. Information they are uncertain about is placed on the Shifting Sands of Doubt. Information that they know they don't know is placed on the Wild Frontiers of Knowledge.

Explain to children that while it is good to be certain of what you know, it is by identifying the Wild Frontiers of Knowledge and investigating them that major discoveries are made.

Let's use an example about space.

Stable Certain Mountains	Shifting Sands of Doubt	Wild Frontiers of Knowledge
Planets	Quantum physics	Dark matter and energy
Asteroids	Acceleration and expansion of the universe	Is there one universe or many?
Gravity	Shape of the universe	Is gravity always the same?
The Milky Way	What caused it?	How big is it?

Games and activities that help children learn to plan

There are a few computer programs that help children to learn planning. Inspiration and Kidspiration can help them to outline and connect ideas or stages. Cogmed provides effective computerised working memory training.

A series of other activities has also been shown to assist children in developing the ability to plan, control their impulses and consider alternatives:

- general exercise, running games, jumping ropes and basketball

- music training
- traditional martial arts training (emphasises self-control discipline and character development)
- Scouts, Cubs, Brownies and Guides
- orienteering and mapping
- theatre sports
- mindfulness training
- completing mazes
- games like chess, backgammon, dominoes, chequers, snap, Monopoly, Battleships and Risk.

Teaching children to consider consequences

Geniuses see connections between things that others don't look for. The realisation that actions have outcomes, consequences and implications is essential to unlocking genius.

Without wanting to sound too metaphysical, a genius sees that everything and everyone is connected. Looking for new and interesting ways things can be connected is part of the way geniuses become creative innovators.

You can help unlock these skills in children by asking them to find ways that things are similar. For example:

- How are a penguin and a dolphin alike?
- How is your foot like a lever?
- How are a mouse and a mountain alike?
- How are the modern world and the Renaissance alike?
- How is the railway system similar to plumbing?

Games like Mousetrap and stories like *This is the house that Jack built* are fun ways to highlight how things are connected.

This is the house that Jack built

by Mother Goose

This is the house that Jack built.
This is the malt that lay in the house that Jack built.
This is the rat that ate the malt
That lay in the house that Jack built.
This is the cat that killed the rat
That ate the malt
That lay in the house that Jack built.
This is the dog
That worried the cat
That killed the rat
That ate the malt
That lay in the house that Jack built.
This is the cow with the crumpled horn
That tossed the dog
That worried the cat
That killed the rat
That ate the malt
That lay in the house that Jack built.
This is the maiden all forlorn
That milked the cow with the crumpled horn
That tossed the dog
That worried the cat
That killed the rat
That ate the malt
That lay in the house that Jack built.
This is the man all tattered and torn
That kissed the maiden all forlorn

That milked the cow with the crumpled horn
That tossed the dog
That worried the cat
That killed the rat
That ate the malt
That lay in the house that Jack built.
This is the priest all shaven and shorn
That married the man all tattered and torn
That kissed the maiden all forlorn
That milked the cow with the crumpled horn
That tossed the dog
That worried the cat
That killed the rat
That ate the malt
That lay in the house that Jack built.
This is the cock that crowed in the morn
That waked the priest all shaven and shorn
That married the man all tattered and torn
That kissed the maiden all forlorn
That milked the cow with the crumpled horn
That tossed the dog
That worried the cat
That killed the rat
That ate the malt
That lay in the house that Jack built.
This is the farmer sowing his corn
That kept the cock that crowed in the morn
That waked the priest all shaven and shorn
That married the man all tattered and torn
That kissed the maiden all forlorn

> That milked the cow with the crumpled horn
> That tossed the dog
> That worried the cat
> That killed the rat
> That ate the malt
> That lay in the house that Jack built.

You can also help children see that consequences and connections are not always certain. One famous example is outlined below.

'Roy,' Mavis says. 'Did you hear about Dave wanting to fly a microlight plane?'

'No, I didn't, Mavis. That's good.'

'No, Roy, that's not good. That was bad. When Dave went up the plane caught fire and he had to jump out.'

'Oh, Mavis,' Roy says. 'That is bad!'

'No, Roy, that's good. He was wearing a parachute.'

'Well, Mavis, that's good.'

'No, Roy,' Mavis says, 'that was bad. The parachute didn't open.'

'Oh, no, Mavis,' Roy says, 'that is definitely bad.'

'Well, no, Roy, that was good. Dave landed on a haystack.'

'Oh, Mavis, that was really good.'

'Uh, well, Roy, that was bad, too. As he was coming down, he spotted a pitchfork sticking up right in the middle of the haystack.'

'Oh, no, Mavis. That was bad.'

'No, Roy, that was good. He missed the pitchfork.'

'Now, Mavis, that's good!'

'Well, no, Roy, that wasn't good either. He also missed the haystack.'

Teaching children to delay gratification

Anyone who has ever smelled something delicious cooking in the kitchen and sneaked a taste before it cooled down knows the value of delaying gratification.

In Chapter 4, the chapter on teaching concentration skills, the focus was on what goes into children's minds. But when teaching planning, you need to focus on output. Selecting an action to take and being able to control the timing of that action is critical to unlocking genius.

Self-control

People who tend to do the first thing that pops into their heads remain scatterbrained and often achieve little.

Some writers have critiqued Walter Mishel's findings from the marshmallow study, suggesting that children who have little reason to trust people would sensibly grab the first marshmallow and gobble it down. The ability to resist the first marshmallow on offer and wait for the second might be more about trust than self-control.

Let's take a bet both ways and think about how you can build trust in your family while also building the ability to delay gratification in your child.

1. You have to follow through. For children to learn that waiting and putting something off is worthwhile they need to feel confident that when a parent says something will happen 'later' that something will actually occur later.

Most parents are good at teaching little children to delay their gratification. It almost comes naturally. Distracting a baby while they are being changed, helping a toddler play with something else while waiting for their turn at the playground or distracting a young child while his or her sister gets ready are all part of most parents' repertoire. To unlock children's genius you need to teach them how to do this, and keep on teaching.

2. Show children how to flex their willpower muscle. This is what my good friend and colleague Professor Lyn Littlefield would call 'Stop, Think, Do'. Stop what you are doing, think about your options and then act accordingly. Games like Simon says, red light, green light and follow the leader are excellent training grounds for these skills.

Teach your child there is a difference between feelings and actions. It is news to some children that just because they feel like a chocolate doesn't mean they always have to have a chocolate. Another example is that it is okay to feel angry but it is not okay to hit.

Some children don't listen well when they suffer from the 'gotta-have-its'. Teach your child to listen well. Get down at their level, speak directly to them and ask them to repeat back to you what you have just said.

3. Geniuses learn how to do the tough, challenging things first. This is how they develop and extend themselves. You can help your child do this by completing study tasks before playing computer games, saving up for things rather than just receiving them and creating progress charts that they can complete as they work towards a goal. Using lay-buy is also a valuable tool.

4. Plan for events. Talk about forthcoming attractions. These can be planned events, birthday parties, Christmas time, holidays. Anticipating and planning for these events helps to build the ability to delay gratification. Projects such as pottery, sculpture, painting, drawing, building models, knitting and weaving also build this skill.

Older children can be given a clothing budget to manage or have their own bank account with their allowance paid in to it each week. The allowance doesn't have to be large but they should be required to keep a minimum balance in their accounts.

Of course we can take all of this delaying gratification too far as well. It is probably not a great idea to delay your dream of climbing Mt Everest until you are 90. If we all waited until we were totally ready before having children the world's population would be in steep decline. That's why the next chapter is about decision-making.

Practising planning with children	
Ages 2–4	■ Talk through your planning out loud to your child, eg 'Now, let's see. First we have to pick up the dry cleaning then we have to buy some lettuce.' ■ Be your word. If you say something is going to happen try as much as you possibly can to make it happen. Trust is essential for children to plan.
Ages 5–7	■ Use mazes and charts. ■ Teach basic music and language skills. ■ Bounce a ball. ■ Skip rope.

	■ Mix paints and colours. ■ Make and decorate a calendar. ■ Grow a garden. ■ Ride a scooter. ■ Follow basic recipes. ■ Cook simple meals. ■ Plan outings. ■ Fly a kite. ■ Playing Simon says and statues. ■ Research topics. Consider what do we need to find out? Where can we find it out from?

Ages 8–11	■ Help children look at the steps and sequence of an issue on sticky notes that they can order and re-order until they can make a plan.
	■ Do mapping activities.
	■ Develop itineraries for trips.
	■ Explore kid-run businesses.
	■ Consider:
	  • Junior Athletics
	  • Little Kickers
	  • Brownies, Cubs
	  • Theatre sports.
	■ Play the card game Switch.
	■ Provide opportunities to do:
	  • Pottery
	  • Sculpture
	  • Painting
	  • Dance
	  • Drawing

	• Model building • Knitting and weaving.

Ages 12–18	■ Involve them in planning family events, holidays and dinners.
	■ Give them a bank account to manage and a clothing budget.
	■ Explore opportunities in:
	  • Yoga and mindfulness training
	  • Theatre sports
	  • Exercise and sports
	  • Skateboarding, skiing, surfing and tobogganing
	  • Orienteering
	  • Caving
	  • Kayaking
	  • Musical performances
	  • Billiards and snooker
	  • Creating playlists of songs
	  • Ropes courses
	  • White-water rafting
	  • Scouts/Guides
	  • Debating
	  • Tapestry
	  • Fashion design
	  • Jewellery-making
	  • Song and music arrangement
	  • Improvisational theatre

CHAPTER 7

Developing the art of decision making

Douglas Adams, the author of The Hitchhiker's Guide to the Galaxy, *once said he wanted to invent a machine that takes our decisions and then tells us the reasons we made them.*

Much of our happiness relates to the decisions we make. Where we live, who we spend time with, what we do, how we approach people, who we are friends with and whether we look after ourselves or not are all dependent on the decisions we make. If we want our children to have happy lives, we have to help them learn to make good decisions.

A good decision increases the likelihood of success. As mentioned in the previous chapter, becoming a good decision maker involves realising that your first idea is not always your best idea and that you should systematically weigh up alternative ways of doing things.

Some decisions are straightforward but they are the exceptions. Making a good decision can be hard work and time consuming. You have to pause, focus your thinking on a particular issue, develop a range of alternatives, weigh up the pros and cons, choose and, most importantly, act on your decision.

Good decision making is an innovative art that takes time to nurture in children. As most people never learn to take that time, they end up selecting between a limited range of options and end up doing the same things over and over again.

In a world that wants to rush us onwards to the fastest decision, the genius stands out because they take their time to make informed, considered and wise decisions.

Turning a decision into action

We can all fall into the trap of making all the decisions for our children and then at a certain age start expecting them to make good decisions for themselves. But if we have never helped them to learn how to make a decision, we shouldn't be overly startled when they make a few blunders.

Lots of people make really good decisions but don't convert their decisions into actions. This can be just as limiting as making a bad decision. It is also very common.

To work out why this happens, let's introduce you to Clyde Beatty.

The fine art of lion taming

In the early to mid-1900s lion taming was not a career that came with a lot of superannuation or retirement benefits. It didn't need to. Most lion tamers met early and nasty ends. Then along came Clyde Beatty.

Clyde Beatty taming a lion with a chair.

At a time when most lion tamers were ending up as food for the lions, Clyde lived to a fine age and had an extraordinary career appearing in films and even had his own radio series. According to James Clear, Clyde managed to survive because he learned one really important skill.

The chair and the whip

As you can see in the photo, Clyde brought into the lion cage a chair and a whip. Now most other lion tamers thought it was the whip that kept the lions under control. It was actually the chair that gave Clyde the edge.

When a chair with four legs is waggled about in front of a lion, the lion doesn't really know which leg to swipe at first. It might have a bit of a go but quickly finds it all too confusing and gives up.

As well as being a bit of handy information should you ever find yourself in a lion cage with a chair close by, it also tells us something about the process of decision-making.

We are all a lot like the lion. When we have too many options we can become bewildered and act on none of the options. Our indecision becomes inactivity or we give up making new choices and resort to the same old ways.

To successfully make a decision we have to have a process that helps us whittle down a few options to just one. Geniuses usually focus their energies on the projects that they have decided to devote time to. The clarity of their decision-making enables them to focus the full weight of their intellectual and creative powers on a specific area.

Teaching your child how to make decisions

Decisions are like crossroads in your life. When you come to a crossroad there are basically five ways you can approach it.

1   Go straight ahead and keep going.
2   Turn left.
3   Turn right.
4   Turn around and go back.
5   Stop and stay where you are.

Crossroads in life

(Yes, I know you could also toss a coin, roll a dice, burrow into the earth or stop to build a space station on the spot and fly into space but let's keep it fairly simple at this stage.)

PICCA

To know which way to go we need to make a decision. To help us remember how to do this it's useful to employ an acronym called **PICCA**, which stands for a five-step way of making decisions.

1   Problem
2   I want
3   Choices
4   Compare
5   Act.

Problem

The first thing to do is to clarify what the problem or decision you need to make is. Generally the need for a decision arises when there is a problem. What's the issue?

At first glance, stating what the problem is may seem very straightforward but it is also important to get it right. For example, a review of the railroad system in 1975 concluded:

> *The railroads did not stop growing because the need for passenger and freight transportation declined. That grew. The railroads are in trouble today not because the need was*

filled by others (cars, trucks, airplanes, even telephones),
but because it was not filled by the railroads themselves.
They let others take customers away from them because
they assumed themselves to be in the railroad business
rather than in the transportation business.

Try out a few different ways of expressing the problem. One of the ways to clarify what the problem is, is to ask yourself five 'why' questions. For example:

1   I'm worried I might fail in my next test at school. *Why?*

2   I haven't studied enough. *Why?*

3   I haven't been sleeping well. *Why?*

4   I've been stressed out. *Why?*

5   I think I will disappoint my parents. *Why?*

I want to give up piano.

In this example the problem to be solved shifts, as it often does, from one thing to another. Problems are shifty things. What sometimes seems to be the problem camouflages the real problem. In the example, the real issue arises that the child doesn't want to disappoint their parents by giving up piano.

Once you have helped your child to identify the problem move to the next stage.

I want

These are also known as objectives but really they are just the things that your child wants. Very few people specify what they want. Or they specify it in such a wishy-washy way that even they are unsure whether they have achieved it. When we clarify what we want, we put our power of intentionality to work. So whether it is 'I want a red bike to ride this summer', or 'I want to live like Ian Fleming (author of the James Bond series) in luxury in Jamaica', write down what you want.

We can help children specify what they want by becoming better at doing this ourselves. One way to do this is to shift from asking people what they want to do to making invitations and proposals. For example, rather than saying to a friend or partner, 'Let's catch up. What would you like to do?' say, 'There's a movie on at the cinema I'd like to see. Would you like to come with me?'

Choices

Have your child describe as many alternative ways of getting what they want as you can. Have a brainstorming session with them if they get stuck.

Take some time on this. It is often best to have children come back to the list of choices three times, adding to it if they can, before they move to the next stage of comparing. Children often develop more ideas standing up than sitting down so perhaps rather than sitting at a desk, place the list on the floor so they can walk around it.

Sometimes choices that we haven't even considered appear if we give ourselves some time to dwell and ponder on the decision. This is why the best decisions take some time.

Compare

Go through the list of choices with children and note which one they really love, which one they think has the best chance and which one is a long shot. If they don't have a long shot option you might encourage them to go back and spend more time developing their choices.

A list of choices that looks too practical and realistic can indicate that they have played too safe in developing possible choices.

Difficult decisions usually have a trade-off, and it's usually not a straightforward matter. For this reason it's worth drawing up a comparison table (as described on pages 121 and 123).

Act

Back to Clyde Beatty. The last thing to do is to help your child select an option and act on it. This means specifying the actions required and developing a time line for completion.

An example of how your child can use PICCA

Emma wants to do an after-school activity this term. She is interested in Girl Guides, piano lessons and gymnastics. Guides meet on Thursday evenings. Piano lessons can be scheduled at any time except when her parents work late on Mondays and Tuesdays, and Wednesdays is the evening her brother Kyle has karate lessons on the other side of town. Gymnastics has a Saturday session as well as one on, you guessed it, Thursday evenings. Friday night is a traditional family evening at home.

Problem

Whether Emma should learn piano, join the Girl Guides or become involved in gymnastics.

I want

Emma makes a list of her 'I wants'.

- I want to meet new friends.
- I want to have fun.
- I want to learn a musical instrument.

Choices

- I could choose either gymnastics or Girl Guides but not both.
- I could ask Granddad to take me to piano lessons on Monday, Tuesday or Wednesday.
- I could learn another instrument at school and piano later.
- I could not do an after-school activity.

Compare

To compare the choices, Emma and her parents draw up a comparison table.

Wants/activities	Piano	Gymnastics	Girl Guides
New friends	No	Yes	Yes
Fun	Yes	Yes	Yes
Musical	Yes	No	No

Still Emma isn't clear on her decision so she decides to give each activity a ranking based on a star system: 3 stars for best, 2 stars for next and 1 star for worst.

Wants/activities	Piano	Gymnastics	Girl Guides
New friends	*	**	***
Fun	***	**	*
Musical	***	*	**
Total	**7 stars**	**5 stars**	**6 stars**

It's a close call. Emma has to spend some time thinking about it. While she really loves the piano, she thinks having more friends is what she wants most. After a while she thinks that maybe having guitar lessons at school would also be okay. Given that she would like to make new friends, Emma thinks she could do this both through the guitar lessons and Girl Guides.

Act

Emma decides to go to Girl Guides on Thursday night.

This might seem like quite a process for Emma to work her way through, but if her parents make every decision for her, she won't learn how to weigh up different options and choose for herself.

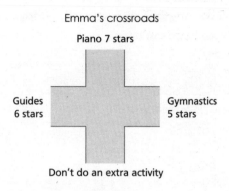

Emma's crossroads

Piano 7 stars

Guides 6 stars

Gymnastics 5 stars

Don't do an extra activity

An example of how parents can use PICCA

George and Judy want to select a school for their young son Elroy.

Problem

The problem is that George and Judy want a school that provides a quality education for Elroy that is near where they live.

I want

To begin with, George and Judy make a list of all the things they would like for Elroy at his potential school.

- Learn the basics.
- Enjoy school.
- Develop creativity.
- Develop discipline.
- Learn good work habits.
- Learn to work with others.
- Participate in physical activities.
- Intellectually challenging.
- Love learning.
- Opportunity to study art.

- Options for the future.
- Long-lasting friendships.
- Basic values.
- Within easy travelling distance.

Choices

There are four schools that would be possible for Elroy to attend: Smithington Grammar School, Whiteside Public School, Eastside School or The Adventure School.

Compare

Here we'll use a 5-star rating system with 5 being optimal and 1 being the worst.

Wants	Smithington Grammar School	Whiteside Public School	Eastside School	The Adventure School
Learn the basics	* * * * *	* * * * *	* * *	* * * * *
Enjoy school	* * *	* * *	* * *	* * * * *
Develop creativity	* *	* * *	* * * * *	* * * * *
Develop discipline	* * * * *	* * * * *	* *	* * *
Learn good work habits	* * * *	* * *	*	* * * *
Learn to work with others	*	* * * *	* * *	* * * * *

Participate in physical activities	***	**	****	*****
Intellectually challenging	*****	*****	**	***
Love learning	**	***	**	*****
Art	***	***	*****	****
Options for the future	*****	****	**	*****
Long-lasting friendships	Unknown	Unknown	Unknown	Unknown
Basic values	*****	*****	***	*****
Easy travelling distance	**	***	*****	**
Total	**45**	**48**	**41**	**56**

George and Judy's crossroads

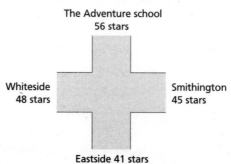

The Adventure school
56 stars

Whiteside
48 stars

Smithington
45 stars

Eastside 41 stars

In terms of meeting the desired characteristics George and Judy conclude the order of schools would be The Adventure School.

Act

Despite being quite a way from their current residence George and Judy decide to enrol Elroy in The Adventure School.

Obviously there are much more complex decision-making models you can access but I find PICCA to be sufficient for most children and fairly easy to work through with them.

Of course, once you have made a decision about the direction you want to go in, it's then a matter of being motivated to start it and stick with it.

Giving children opportunities to make decisions	
Ages 2–4	<ul><li>To feel safe, young children need to know that you are making the major decisions for them. Talk to them about the decisions you are making, reason out loud in front of them, model changing your mind and re-evaluating a decision from time to time.</li><li>Care for pets.</li><li>Create gardens.</li><li>Get involved in basic gymnastics.</li><li>Give them choices (at times).</li><li>Ask them to suggest some parts of the dinner menu.</li></ul>
Ages 5–7	<ul><li>Help with setting the table.</li><li>Cooking basic meals.</li><li>Grow and eat vegetables.</li><li>Act out historical characters.</li><li>Play:<ul><li>Hockey</li></ul></li></ul>

	• Football • Mouse Trap • Solitaire • Scrabble Junior • Chinese chequers • Chess. ■ Plan sleepovers.
Ages 8–11	■ These are the critical years to be working through PICCA with children. Use it to model decisions that are facing you and let them see you consciously plan. ■ As situations arise in their own life, see them as opportunities for them to learn about planning and decision-making. Be patient as they go through this. It can take a while for children to systematically go about making a decision rather than just jumping into the first solution they can find. ■ Create your own adventure books. ■ Try sailing. ■ Play Uno. ■ Tackle junior electronic kits. ■ Try mountain bike riding and canoeing.
Ages 12–18	■ Some teenagers will want to make all of the decisions for you. How much to spend on them, what time they should go to bed, how much their allowance should be and so on. ■ Not all your decisions and negotiations may be smooth ones at this stage. If you use PICCA to guide you through, at least you will be modelling a considered

way of making decisions. You and your teenager may come up with different evaluations of choices. Over critical issues your decision will need to prevail. While it is occasionally good for teenagers to feel that they have convinced their parents, parents mainly need to be in charge.

- Get involved in debating.
- Try acting and drama classes, Tae Kwon Do, rafting, Dungeons and Dragons, dirt bike riding or skate parks.

CHAPTER 8

Motivation, persistence and grit

Failure is the opportunity to begin again, this time more intelligently.

Henry Ford

Geniuses keep on going when others give up. There are four laws of success.

1 You can't succeed at something you never try doing.
2 You can't succeed at something unless you are prepared to keep trying to improve at it until you succeed.
3 When you feel reluctant to try something, remember rule 1.
4 When you want to give up on something, remember rule 2.

Pretty basic, isn't it? And yet the number of people who spend their lives searching for that elusive revving-up agent called motivation is amazing. Once they gain that elusive thing called motivation they will give it to all their children, amaze their friends and family by rising in the morning as chirpy as a songbird before taking on the tasks of the day with gusto. They will become a pumped-up human whirlwind.

The impetus towards genius lies within. So let's talk about helping children acquire the motivation and drive they will need. What do you think are the best predictors of success in schools and careers?

IQ? *No.*
Luck? *No.*

Talent? *No.*
Where you were born? *No.*
What school you went to? *No.*

The strongest single predictor of success is your level of persistence. Moreover, developing self-discipline is a higher predictor of academic results and improvements in grade scores.

Learning the lessons of computer game design

I have never yet met a child who has said, 'I am not motivated to go to the next level of Call of Duty/World of Warcraft/(insert the name of almost any computer game you like).'

Computer game designers know a lot about what motivates, engages and keeps the interest of children. You probably remember the first generation of computer games – Pong, Space Invaders, Frogger and others. These games were designed in such a way that if a player lost, they would have to restart the game. The problem was, the computer game designers found that boys would only play for three times before giving up. If a boy lost or had to restart a game on three consecutive occasions he would say, 'This game is stupid' and give up.

As you can imagine, this wasn't great news for the computer game designers. So they set about reinventing their games. The most recent computer games have numbers of different levels, you gain points, skills, tools and weapons as you continue on in the game, and most have some social interaction and connectivity.

The computer game designers had learned the lessons of the great behavioural psychologist BF Skinner. If you want someone to keep doing something, dangle success just in front of their nose and make sure the reward is attainable but not guaranteed to occur every time.

So how can parents incorporate the sheer cunning of BF Skinner and the designers of World of Warcraft into family life? In the following section I look at some general lessons you can learn from computer games then relate these to coaching and inspiring your child's genius.

Lesson 1: Success needs to occur within three tries

After three unsuccessful attempts at anything children can become demotivated and give up. Try to give children at least a sense of improvement within their first three tries at anything. Acknowledge the challenge and comment on something they are progressing well in.

Lesson 2: Knowledge is not just acquired but is used almost immediately

In most computer games you don't gain some information and have to store it later, just in case it might turn out to be useful. Almost always you get to use that new piece of knowledge immediately.

Lesson 3: Rapid, self-scoring feedback is used to help refine successful strategies

Feedback comes fast in computer games and is used to change the approach the player makes to the game.

Lesson 4: Make 'having a go' risk free

In most computer games players are placed in situations where they can take risks while real life consequences are lowered.

Lesson 5: Mirroring effect

Children are allowed to take on adult-like roles and experience a sense of success. This is not confined, of course, to computer games.

Many of the great works of children's literature – *Tom Sawyer, The Magic Faraway Tree, Harry Potter, Swallows and Amazons* – all feature children taking on adult-like roles without adult supervision.

Lesson 6: People seek out challenges especially if they are thought of as fun

If we look around at the world of people playing cards and sudoku or completing crosswords, it is clear that people love a challenge. When we call it fun or play rather than work people will do it for hours on end.

In India the kite-flying craze 'patang baazi' has children planning strategies and counter-manoeuvres with a level of focus that most military generals would admire.

Lesson 7: Success is contagious!

A sense of belonging can be promoted through shared activities. The more recent computer games build a social network through sharing ideas with other players or competing against them. This allows players to talk about their successes and to also feel even more successful when they can share tips or 'cheats' with other players.

This is true beyond the world of computers. If children get a feeling of success, they tend to seek out more of it.

Lesson 8: Build and use dopamine

The neurochemical dopamine is related to our sense of motivation Computer games build up dopamine through a combination of challenges and rewards with repetitive moments.

While not everything can be turned into a game, knowing that children love challenges when it is safe to have a go, where there is a sense of playfulness and where there is always a chance to have another turn is useful knowledge for parents. Playing guessing games, Trivial Pursuit, board games and flying a kite are all powerful examples of building motivation. The main idea is to focus on playing in the moment rather than thinking about the result.

Positive coaching

Let's visit the godfather of modern coaching, Timothy Gallwey. Timothy, a tennis coach, realised that his mindfulness studies with Indian Guru Maharaj Ji had application to coaching people to perform at their best.

In almost any human activity there are two processes going on at the same time. An external one in which we contend with challenges from the environment and an inner process where we have to overcome our doubts and beliefs about our abilities.

Timothy noticed that giving a player a specific instruction such as, 'Wait until the ball is close to the baseline and when it bounces at its highest point, hit a return shot,' did not result in an improvement in their playing. In fact his players often got so focused on trying to follow his instructions, their level of playing declined.

Fear + Worry = Loss of awareness = Loss of motivation

Timothy decided to change the focus of his coaching from issuing instructions and giving constructive feedback to increasing awareness. What his players needed to succeed wasn't more pressure or information: it was more presence and more awareness. Instead of giving an instruction, Gallwey asked his players, 'Can you say bounce out loud when the ball bounces and hit out loud when you hit the ball?' He found that the players' performance increased dramatically once they focused on the immediate task at hand.

Timothy Gallwey was coaching very skilled players, many of whom were so focused on critically evaluating their playing style they didn't perform at their best. Parents also often have children who are capable of genius but instead spend their time being self-critical and limiting their success.

Motivation has more to do with children overcoming their fears than anything else. It can feel much easier to not put in effort than to risk failing at something. Fears loom larger if we try to avoid them.

Shift children's attention away from achieving an outcome towards the process of what they are doing right now. This means being non-judgemental about the performance.

The best learning happens when we are focusing on what we are doing right now. This is true when children play.

The more you try to succeed the more likely you are to fail. The reason is that when we try hard we shift our awareness away from what we are doing to the outcome.

In sport this is why you see players choke and miss easy shots. This is why you see trainee musicians rush through difficult parts of a piece. They lose their focus on what they are doing right now and begin to focus on the outcome.

Helping children use a system to stay motivated at school

In working with thousands of high performing sixth form students, one feature of their success stands out above all others – they develop a system. That system tells them when to study and when to rest and they follow the system whether they feel like it or not. Teach children that systems are more important than goals.

Geniuses work out systems that work for them. You can help your child to work out when is the best time to play, to read, to watch television and to go to bed. This can be helpful to do around the rush hours that afflict most families – getting out the door in the morning and getting everyone into bed on time at night.

Systems are better than goals. Setting goals for yourself and for your children is fine but if they get so focused on the goal they can become anxious. Alternatively, the goals we set can limit us. For example, if you set a goal of losing 5 kilograms and achieve it, you might then stop eating and living healthily and put on all the weight you had lost.

Of course, no system works all the time. The morning comes when you just can't get out of bed to go to the gym. The healthy diet gets a beating from the chocolate cake. You just don't have the energy to do homework tonight.

The answer is … return to the system. You might have missed a day but have a family policy of 'we don't miss twice'.

Students often find it harder to remain motivated in the second half of the school year. The most important thing to remind your child is that a lull in motivation hasn't really got much to do with a lack of motivation. It has more to do with feeling anxious and worried.

Genius is strengthened by a mid-year tune up and rev up. It is an excellent time to focus your child's awareness using the following techniques.

Set small goals and one large one

Let's discuss the most powerful self-motivation techniques. For each subject that your child does at school, set a small goal each week. For example, a goal might be to read and understand a chapter of their reading book. Write the goal down and place it somewhere both you and your child can see it. When your child has achieved that goal give it a tick. Just the sense of completion involving in ticking off a completed task increases motivation.

Ask children to make their favourite subject at school the one that they will go for broke in. In this subject the aim is to top the class. This is the subject that they will use to judge themselves by. Children feel that narrowing the focus to one main school subject is an achievable goal.

Get them organised

Get up to date. Even geniuses miss deadlines. If your child has fallen behind in any subject, have a working bee to catch up. I know there is a part of any parent that thinks, 'Well, if you didn't muck around so much, you wouldn't need to be catching up now. It's your own fault. Why should I now help you to catch up?' Ditch the anger and the payback and pitch in. This is particularly important in the senior years of schooling. The following suggestions might help.

- Children can ask teachers to help them by saying something like, 'I lost motivation for a while in this subject but now I'd really like to catch up.'
- If they have not been in the practice of taking notes, help them to start. If they've missed notes, ask for copies of them.
- If they have become embarrassed about asking questions in class, set a goal of asking one question per class. If that is too embarrassing for children, encourage them to ask the teacher after class. If even that is too embarrassing, ask them to email their teacher.
- Write a revision summary for the subject to date topic by topic.
- If the actual study area has become a mess, help them to clean it up.

Realise this process may take some time with your child. You wouldn't expect anyone to enter a marathon without doing a series of shorter training runs first and the same thing applies to your child doing well at school. Regaining their motivation is a step-by-step process.

Help them give up focusing on everyone else

Even very clever children who feel unmotivated think everyone else knows more, is more talented, is smarter and has a lot more brains than they do. Most students have absolutely no idea how well they are doing at school.

As I talked about in the David and Goliath example (see Chapter 3), the main thing is to help children play to their own mix of strengths.

Help your child to use their time in school well

Many children muck around in school and then wonder why they have to do so much work outside of school. Ask your children to sit towards the front in class. If they can focus and listen well while at school they can save themselves endless hours. This is valuable time saved that can be later used for hanging out with friends and having fun.

Build honesty

If your child has felt unmotivated they may have done anything to avoid doing the study time. The world is full of excuses that can be made: 'The dog needs a walk' or 'I have to finish this game and then I'll study.' You have to be tough enough to insist that your children do the work **BEFORE** they play the computer game/watch TV/go online to chat.

Also help children to be honest enough to admit to themselves that lying in bed with the computer on, listening to music with a DVD on in the background and messenger open to chat with friends is not and will never be, studying. During study time ensure they're sitting up at a desk or table with **NO** electronic distractions.

Build a new system

If your child has been finding it difficult to get motivated, build a new system. For example, study in a local library rather than at home or change the room they study in.

Tell your child that just as you learn to skate best by skateboarding, you learn to succeed in exams and essays by giving your undivided attention to your study. Have them practise in the same conditions they intend to perform in. There won't be electronics and music in the exam room.

Deal with self-sabotage

Your child might be able to dismiss all of the above points by saying 'I can't do it' or 'I can't be bothered' or 'This sucks'. That is just the part of them that is scared, talking them out of it. This is Rex talking Albert out of it. Rex has detected a threat and thinks that if you try and fail, it will be much worse than never having tried in the first place.

Think about what would happen if children applied this type of thinking to the whole of their life. They wouldn't learn music and start a band because Cold Play, Taylor Swift and Jay-Z have already done it. They wouldn't talk to someone they like because they would be rejected. They wouldn't go to a place they would really like because it would probably disappoint them. They wouldn't live the life they could live because they would lack the daring and courage. See Chapter 9 for more on teaching children to have a go.

Give up fear and gain motivation

You know the number one fear of all time for children? Death? *No.* Speaking in public? *No.*

The number one fear that people have is that other people will think badly of them. And you know what the biggest and saddest joke about that fear is?

Most people don't think about others at all. Most people are so busy or so focused on themselves they haven't got the interest or the energy to judge whether you are good at something or not.

There is a chance that your child could throw away a really successful, enjoyable life by worrying about something that doesn't even exist. So as Yoda in *Star Wars* said, 'There is only do or not do; there is no try.' *Don't let your child make what other people might think of them if they stuff up a reason for giving up on themselves.*

Follow your passions

Geniuses find areas that they are passionate about and pursue them relentlessly, often without thought of reward of recognition. For geniuses the passion and the accomplishment is its own reward. When Howard Florey, a man who has likely saved your life, found a way to administer penicillin to effectively treat bacterial infections, his motivation was to alleviate human misery. Similarly, Professor Fiona Wood in 1999 developed a spray-on skin to treat burns victims. Fiona and her team in Perth played a key role in treating burns victims from the 2002 Bali bombings.

One of the best pieces of career advice you can give your children to increase their motivation is to tell them to find their passion and go and do it.

Keep on keeping on	
Ages 2–4	■ Play, laugh, have fun.
	■ Focus on hands-on real world exploration.
	■ Emphasise experiences that involve all the senses – touch, balance, sight, sound, smell and at times taste.
	■ Play hide and seek.
	■ Follow mystery trails around the garden.
	■ Make learning playful and fun.
	■ Make a family ritual of going out and finding out about things.
	■ Make collections – flowers, seashells, pebbles, stickers, pictures.
	■ Read every day.

Ages 5–7	<ul><li>Play guessing games.</li><li>Enjoy kite-flying.</li><li>Encourage simple puzzles and games, play jigsaws, spot the difference and build with blocks.</li><li>Rhythmic movements to increase dopamine:<ul><li>dancing</li><li>percussion</li><li>belly dancing and body maths.</li></ul></li><li>Read Dr. Seuss's book, *Oh, the places you'll go!*</li></ul>
Ages 8–11	<ul><li>Play handball, basketball, volleyball, ping pong, badminton or gymnastics.</li><li>Swim.</li><li>Play the drums.</li><li>Focus on the process not the outcome.</li><li>Develop daily schedules and routines (systems).</li><li>Set several small goals and one large one.</li><li>Limit screen time.</li><li>Be on a treasure hunt for passions and interests.</li><li>Theatre sports.</li><li>Find-the-word games.</li><li>Find the next number games.</li><li>Pottery, sculpture and art.</li><li>Help kids to conduct investigations into areas of interest where the answer leads to another question. For example:<ul><li>Why did dinosaurs die out?</li><li>Was it a massive explosion?</li><li>Was it worldwide climate change?</li><li>If they died out why didn't crocodiles and alligators?</li></ul></li></ul>

	• If they didn't die out, did they become something else? • Are dinosaurs now birds?
Ages 12–18	■ Develop systems. ■ Find an area they are passionately interested in and help them to succeed using Timothy Gallwey's methods. ■ Try team sports as well as challenging individual sports such as skiing, surfing, rock climbing, BMX bike riding. ■ Teach them to analyse their systems to find out whether the outcome is positive or negative. ■ Keep them organised and up to date. ■ Renegotiate the daily schedule but keep having one. ■ Continue to limit screen time. ■ Complete study tasks before playing computer games. ■ Keep expanding their worlds by going to different places, doing different things and continuing to expand their minds. ■ Help them to learn to write down goals. ■ Help them to use their time in school well. ■ Build on their strengths. ■ Build honesty and discourage excuses. ■ Get involved in improvisational theatre.

CHAPTER 9

Building a can-do mindset – the psychology of genius

If it wasn't for me, I would do brilliantly.

Chamfort

Have you ever heard children say, 'This is too hard', 'I'm not good at this', 'I can't be bothered', 'I'm bored and tired'? They have taken on an *I can't do it* mindset. Have you ever seen a child who is highly capable in one area but underestimates his or her ability to do many other things?

No matter how clever, capable and brilliant children are, the risk is they will never really unlock their own genius because they talk themselves out of having a go. Their own attitudes sabotage their chances of creating a great life.

It took research almost 90 years to prove Henry Ford correct when he said, 'Whether you think you can, or you think you can't, either way you are right.' Research by Albert Bandura on self-efficacy, and Carol Dweck on fixed and growth mindsets, proved Henry right.

One of the most powerful things you can do to create great outcomes in your children's lives is to help them develop a can-do mindset.

To do this I need to introduce you to Herbert Marsh. Herbert is a Professor of Educational Psychology who identified that children have two types of self-efficacy: global and specific. Global refers to the way you view yourself as a good person. Specific refers to your prediction of your ability to do something such as ride a bike, finish secondary school or dance the tango. There are as many specific self-competencies as there are things to do.

Child-rearing experts used to think that if children could be helped to feel globally good about themselves their confidence in completing specific tasks would improve. What Professor Marsh discovered was that precisely the reverse is true. If you can help a child to feel able and confident in one specific area this can ricochet positively into other areas of life.

The big news here is that if you go on a treasure hunt and find skills and abilities in your children and help them to challenge themselves even more in that area, you will improve their confidence and their positive mindset overall. If children have a go and you notice their efforts, they develop a positive attitude towards improvement.

Research on neuroplasticity tells us our children's brains can get smarter when they work at it. Despite all of this research, human beings often seem resolutely determined to put themselves down, talk themselves out of things, be fearful of trying new things and generally act in ways that lock up rather than unlock their genius. To understand that we need to turn to fleas. What the? But yes, read on …

What we can learn from fleas

Most people have heard of the glass ceiling effect from feminist literature. The idea is that there is an imaginary glass ceiling that stops many women aspiring to the top positions in organisations. Few people know where the term 'glass ceiling' came from.

Did you know that fleas can jump 100 times their own height into the air? That's the equivalent of a 1.8 metre person jumping 180 metres. But if you placed some fleas into a cardboard box and put a piece of glass over the top of the box and left it there for a few days, you would learn something amazing. When you came back and lifted the glass off, the fleas, despite still being able to jump 100 times their own height, would only jump as high as where the glass was placed. The fleas have forgotten what they are capable of.

I hopefully won't offend you when I tell you that your child is like a flea. Like the fleas, children can forget what they are capable of. They take on beliefs about their limitations – and develop their own glass ceiling.

As a parent who wants to help their child reach their true potential, you need to lift the lid on their heads and peer inside to look at the sorts of ideas and thoughts flying around in there. And that takes us back to our old friends Rex and Albert (see Chapter 2).

Albert thoughts and Rex thoughts

We have all kinds of thoughts flying through our heads all the time. Some of those thoughts are sheer genius. Other thoughts should be taken out the back and quietly thrown away.

It is a day of enlightenment for most of us when we finally realise that not all of our thoughts are equally reliable. Children and teenagers don't know this. Most of them believe that all their thoughts are true.

Help your child to understand that there are two main types of thoughts: Albert thoughts and Rex thoughts. Rex thoughts are the negative ideas that circle around and eat up our confidence and optimism. Albert thoughts are more positive and helpful.

When a pessimistic child starts expressing a lot of Rex thoughts it can be useful to pull them up and say something like, 'Okay I've just heard ten Rex thoughts in a row. Now let's hear a few Alberts.'

It will take a while for a child to learn the difference between Rex and Albert thoughts but you've got time. Children tend to believe their own thoughts absolutely and also hear criticisms very literally, so learning to weigh up different ideas can take time. You can teach your children about this at any age, but it may take until they are eight or nine years of age before it really takes hold.

Examples of Rex and Albert thoughts	
Rex	**Albert**
I can't draw well.	I could learn and improve.
I can't play music.	I could play music if I wanted to but I'm not interested.
I get stressed in tests and exams.	Everyone gets a bit stressed and anyway it prepares me to do my best.
I feel nervous when I go and speak to new people.	Everyone gets a bit nervous meeting people for the first time and all of my friends now were strangers once.

You may wonder why we have Rex thoughts at all if they are so negative and limiting. Rex helps you and helped your ancestors to survive. Rex is the reason you are here breathing and holding this book. You see, we are all the descendants of cautious, paranoid pessimists.

Your ancestors weren't the type of people who thought, 'Ah there might be a sabre tooth tiger in those bushes over there but let's not worry about it.' No. Those were the people who got eaten up. It was the cautious, paranoid pessimists who moved to safer territory as soon as they heard the rustling of a bush who survived to eventually produce you.

Humans pay more attention to threats and negative (or Rex) thoughts rather than positive (or Albert) thoughts because this is what helped them to survive.

You can't avoid having Rex thoughts. Just when you think you have attained that lofty, serene place of enlightenment a Rex thought swims through your head to remind you that you are just as vulnerable and as human as all the rest of us.

Given that most of us will have many more Rex thoughts than Albert thoughts, unless we learn to convert Rex thoughts into Albert thoughts we get stuck, give up, become despondent and resign ourselves to a bleak future.

Getting to know our Rex thoughts

Rex thoughts keep us comfortable and safe but they also dim the lights on our genius and our success. They lead us to do things that direct our energies away from what we want to do. If you look around the world you will see a lot of people doing a lot of things to *not* solve the problems they are facing. For example, gambling, drinking and comfort eating are just some of the ways people can distract themselves.

Whether it is a child having a massive temper tantrum after being good all day at school or a student worrying at night about an exam the next morning, neither of these actions is likely to solve their problems. In fact they may just make them worse. Let's have a look at two common examples of what a Rex thought can do.

Sarah loves school and wants to do well but has a Rex thought that she must never do badly on a test. (Note that Rex thoughts are sneaky: never is a big word and what actually constitutes doing badly is not precisely defined in Sarah's mind.)

Of course the inevitable day comes when Sarah gets a C on a test. A Rex attack occurs and Sarah goes over and over the test in her mind and torments herself into an anxious state. To try to get out of that feeling she blames the teacher and thinks the teacher must have been grumpy and mean when she marked the test. That doesn't really sit well with Sarah. Generally she likes and trusts her teacher. Sarah feels bad about getting a C, but rather than analysing what lessons she can learn from this for her future she tries to alleviate her bad feelings by being overly nice and helpful to other people.

If she doesn't do something to tackle her Rex thoughts, Sarah may lead a life where she becomes a people-pleaser who sacrifices her own needs for those of others and who facilitates other people to shine while she plays a supportive role.

Jimmy also likes school and, like Sarah, he's smart. One day a few of his classmates make fun of him for asking a question in class. At first he's a bit confused and shrugs it off but his friends keep taunting him. He's upset, but he doesn't say anything as he's worried that he will lose his friends.

He assumes that what is a problem today will always be a problem. Jimmy wants to be popular so he starts adopting his classmate's attitudes. He gives up asking questions in class and pretends so well that he finds school boring that he starts to believe it. Rex thoughts like these lead innumerable smart boys and girls to act in stupid ways and fail at school.

We all have Rex thoughts. But geniuses recognise when their primitive brains are sabotaging them and don't let those ideas stop them. When you become aware of the sorts of Rex thoughts your child has they are in a better position to stage a counterattack and give Albert some room to emerge.

In the table on the next page, circle all of the ways your child sometimes sabotages his or her success because of Rex thoughts, then ask yourself the following questions:

- In what way are these strategies working for your child?
- What do you think the strategies they are using might be costing them?
- What are some alternative things they could be doing?

Circle all of the ways your child sometimes sabotages their success				
Finds faults in things	Blames someone else	Blaming him/herself	Makes it worse than it is	Gossips
Complains to someone who can't solve the problem	Turns someone into an enemy	Clams up and doesn't talk about it	Pretends there isn't a problem	Thinks saying something will upset other people
Rescues others	Becomes overly helpful or considerate	Goes over and over the problem	Expects that life will always be difficult	Thinks the problem will always be a problem
Becomes upset over irrelevant details	Vows revenge	Procrastinates (puts things off)	Works too hard	Tries to do things perfectly
Sleeps less	Changes his/her eating patterns	Changes his/her exercise patterns	Either doesn't see friends or sees them too much	Tries to forget or not think about the problem
Makes jokes	Decides it's too much trouble	Gives up and does something else	Tells him/herself he/she didn't like it anyway	Distracts him/herself by doing things completely unrelated to the problem

How to stop Rex assassinating your child's genius

Rex won't give up of his own accord. You will need to teach your child ways to challenge and defeat him, to notice when they are doing some of the strategies from the table on the previous page and think about whether that is working for them.

You have a powerful role in supporting your child's Albert thoughts and helping them to fend off Rex thoughts. Some strategies are outlined below.

'Get to' and 'yet'

When it comes to helping children to unlock their genius, I find two phrases are crucial – **GET TO** and **YET.**

Shifting language from 'I have to' to 'I get to' helps all of us to be more grateful and appreciate the wonderful opportunity of being alive. We all fall into the trap of the 'have-to's': 'I have to go to work', 'I have to get the car serviced' or ' I have to finish this project'. The next time you find yourself doing the 'have-to's' try to stop, consider and turn it into a 'get-to': 'I get to go to work', 'I get to service my car', or 'I get to finish this project'.

Of the estimated 107,602,707,791 people to have lived on earth, only 8 billion or approximately 7.4 per cent are alive right now. Think for a moment of all of your ancestors who would give almost anything to be doing what you are doing right now.

When Rex gets going you might hear your child say things like, 'I'm no good at numbers' or 'I can't play piano' or 'I'm not creative'. There will be times when you want to discuss this in detail with them but on other occasions you could just add the word 'yet': 'You are no good at numbers – yet.' The addition of one little word can alter a child's whole mindset.

Look for opportunities more than threats

A father once gave his two sons different presents. One of his sons received a valuable gold watch and the other a pile of horse manure. The son who received the gold watch came in with a worried look concerned about how to keep his new watch safe. The other son bounded in and said, 'Wow, thanks for the pony, Dad, now I've just got to find it!'

Our perspective matters. It's the difference between going to an event and seeing if it's fun or deciding to have fun when you go to an event. The second attitude is most likely to lead to a happier life.

Teach your child to extract the gold out of life's experiences. Some questions you might ask to help them find the gold are:

- What can we learn from this?
- Setbacks are tough but they teach us to succeed next time. What do you think we need to change?
- What parts of it did you like?

Rex is a tough, wily opponent so you need to be resolute in your determination to highlight opportunities that are possible and lessons that can be learned.

There is no 'try'

You need to help your children adopt a language of integrity. Excuses are lies. They are little stories we make up to sell ourselves out of having a great life. As such they should be treated with scepticism and disdain.

In most areas of life you either choose something or you do not. When you insist your children choose and create their lives, this leads to a sense of empowerment.

You need to apply this language to yourself as well. This means a low tolerance for your own excuses and also being prepared to model that you are choosing to do the things you do.

Too many potential geniuses wallow around in the quagmire of excuses, letting themselves off the hook and living 'could-a-been' lives.

To praise or not to praise – the fine art of giving feedback

This is a vexed issue. We all want our children to feel good about themselves, to know that we love them and believe in them. We also know from the harsh lessons of our own lives that the world does not automatically praise you every time you try to do something.

If you focus only on your child's capabilities you can inadvertently create a sense of cautiousness and an unwillingness to try things that they feel they may not succeed at.

To deny your child the sense that you think they are wonderful and are capable of doing wonderful things in the world seems too harsh so here is a way of straddling that fine line. Remind your child from time to time that you think they are a genius but they just don't know that for themselves yet. Then direct the vast bulk of your positive comments and feedback to the effort they make towards achieving a good result.

Make statements about effort like:

- I'm impressed you worked really hard at that.
- It's great that you practised that piano piece; it's really coming together.
- You can really tell that all the work you've put into this is paying off.

Building a positive approach to life	
Ages 2–4	<ul><li>Be by their side as they explore the world.</li><li>Be ready to marvel and wonder at the magic they see, which adults all too often miss.</li></ul>

	<ul><li>One of the greatest things about being a parent or grandparent is you get to be a kid again and see life, beauty and joy as a child sees it.</li><li>Praise in terms of efforts made rather than outcomes accomplished.</li><li>Start using the terms 'get to' and 'yet'.</li><li>Swim.</li><li>Play with kaleidoscopes.</li></ul>
Ages 5–7	<ul><li>Talk about helpful and unhelpful thoughts – some children like to describe these as Rex and Albert thoughts.</li><li>Throughout these years, follow a simple parenting policy: let them know you think they are great, remind them they are capable of great genius and that you believe in them (refer to the parenting message at the beginning of this book). Then make the most of your feedback and comments about the effort they put in by complimenting and acknowledging them.</li></ul>
Ages 8–11	<ul><li>Talk about how we can sabotage our own success at times.</li><li>Explain Albert thoughts and Rex thoughts and how we all have them and how we can tackle them.</li><li>Be caring and compassionate but don't dwell too long on problems. Move the conversation to opportunities and solutions as soon as you can.</li><li>Build a 'can-do' attitude in your family home. Try to discuss possibilities more than limitations. This doesn't mean that you become a slave to your child. For example, if they come home from school and say,</li></ul>

	'I want to go to India,' you might reply, 'Terrific idea. Let's work out a way to save up enough money to do that.' If they come home and say, 'I want frog legs and ice-cream for dinner,' you might reply, 'Great! You find the frogs. I've got the ice-cream.'
Ages 12–18	■ Teenagers are acutely aware of whether they fit in or not. They can be dramatically despairing and flamboyantly give up on things at times. They can also use the same spirit to take up things.
	■ Don't get too swept up in the highs and lows of teenage moods and dramas. Instead calmly and positively stick to your policy of commenting on and acknowledging effort.
	■ Help them to analyse the system regardless of whether the outcome was what they wanted or not.
	■ Keep using the terms 'get to' and 'yet.'
	■ Play with optical illusions, mind tricks and mazes.

CHAPTER 10

Imagination, creativity and problem-solving

If I'd asked people what they wanted, they would have said faster horses.

Henry Ford

Knowledge is a love affair with answers. Creativity and wisdom are love affairs with questions and possibilities.

Creativity is highly predictive of success in later life but sadly, research tells us that children are becoming less creative. In a world where creativity is possibly diminishing, parents wishing to unlock their children's genius need to consider ways to stimulate their creativity.

More creative ideas occur in the bath or shower, after sleeping or on long rambling walks than anywhere else. Relaxing your way to genius might seem strange but it works. When Archimedes cried out 'Eureka!' (Greek for 'I've found it') in the bath, it is likely a change in his brain waves from relaxing was partly responsible.

There are many examples of inventive solutions to problems being found when people were focused on relaxing. Ludwig van Beethoven, Carl Jung, Wolfgang Mozart and John Ruskin often came across great ideas when walking after a meal. Leonardo da Vinci would stare at a wall until forms took shape in his head. Charles Darwin walked a mile-long thinking path. He would place a pile of stones at the start and at the completion of each lap would kick away one stone until he came across an idea. Albert Einstein played the violin and sailed in order to feel the forces of nature and to seek out inspiration.

When we talk about concentration we often think of sharpening our focus, but creative thinking often involves a broadening and softening of our focus.

Being able to look at something afresh enables people to ask fresh questions. This is why scientists did not make all of our great scientific discoveries. For example Joseph Priestly, who discovered oxygen in 1774, was a minister. Pierre de Fermat, whose last theorem puzzled mathematicians for centuries, was a lawyer. Benjamin Franklin, who invented spectacles, was a politician, diplomat and printer.

Knowledge and interest are important but to see links that others can't you need a dreamy, flexible shifting of ideas. New perspectives emerge when you embrace that simple genius skill of knowing an idea but not holding it too tightly.

Many young children start asking questions that not many people bother to ask such as 'Why do ducks quack?' and 'Why is grass green?' but learn early on not to bother busy adults with so many questions.

Often by about seven or eight years of age children have become self-conscious and ashamed of asking questions and not knowing. The tragedy is this is precisely the time of life when children are able to begin thinking abstractly about things. If they have an adult to help guide them, someone who suggests looking at situations from varying perspectives, they develop mental flexibility.

You can encourage free-range thinking by focusing on the similarities and connections between ideas rather than the categories they belong to. For example, you could quickly discuss how sunshine, rain, sleet, snow, storms and wind are all aspects of a category we could call weather or you could have a discussion with children about how all of these are linked.

Mind stretching for beginners

When Dutch chess master Jan Hein Donner was asked how he would prepare for a chess match against a computer like IBM's Deep Blue, Donner replied, 'I would bring a hammer.'

Mind stretching might sound a bit painful but it is playful and fun. It is about taking ideas and pulling and twisting them out of shape to see if they fit somewhere else.

Thinking weird ideas may cause people to look oddly at you, but it also brings about the sparks of genius. When Christopher Cockerell invented the hovercraft in 1956 he combined the ideas of a plane and a boat floating on air and travelling over the sea. The first person to invent a tap that could provide running water must have been viewed sceptically at first.

Arthur Koestler defined creativity as the defeat of habit by originality. Helping children to look freshly at commonplace objects and to consider different uses for them helps stretch minds. Trying out new perspectives gives us more choice over how we respond to situations and makes change more possible.

Stop the divide!

There is a crazy idea that there are people who were just born creative and others who are not. We might convey this message to our children if we describe ourselves as 'not artistic'. It is easy for us to transmit our own anxieties and limitations to our children. The next time you catch yourself saying, 'I'm not musical', 'I'm not good at mathematics' or 'I was never any good at school' at least add 'but my child can be'.

What stops people being creative?

- Beliefs that there are creative and non-creative people.
- Being told to do something productive.
- Sarcasm.
- Criticism.
- A belief that if one child in a family is good at something that is his or her area and others can't succeed in that interest.
- Pressure to succeed.
- Being laughed at.
- Being made fun of.
- Overeagerness and focusing on the results.
- Rankings at school and comparing yourself with others.

Thinking routines for creativity

Becoming more creative is something we can develop in ourselves and our children. Creativity is within everyone's grasp – it just needs to be given time and encouragement to develop.

Walt Disney had three rooms in which he used to come up with creative thoughts. In the first he was a dreamer combining new ideas; in the second, a realist looking at the shortcomings of an idea. In the third room he was a critic where he would consider if the idea had entertainment value and whether it could be done even better. Edward de Bono developed a system of using six different coloured thinking hats: red for feelings; black for cautions; yellow for benefits; green for creativity; white for facts; and blue for process.

The process of creativity is one of spark and sift. Sparking new ideas is exciting but sifting and revealing the great ideas from the not-so-great may be even more important.

Be aware of difficulties

Notice the things that irritate you and other people. About 50 years ago, IKEA employee Gillis Lungren had a problem. He was trying to fit a table into the boot of his car. By taking the legs off the table and lying it flat in the boot he found it fitted. In doing so he inadvertently invented the flat packaging now used by IKEA. Assume there is a missed opportunity because there usually is.

In 1995 Pierre Omiday was considering how auctions worked and combined it with the internet to create eBay. What object is as unimaginable as the internet was in 1980?

Develop curiosity

Curiosity comes naturally to children. What stifles it is fear of failure and making mistakes. Have a family policy that there is no such thing as failure. There is only feedback.

Terrific training is available for developing children's curiosity about how ideas can be played with. It is called comedy. The Marx brothers, Abbot and Costello, *Seinfeld, Blackadder, The Simpsons, Family Guy, South Park, Anchor Man, Shaun the Sheep* all provide great examples of ideas being stretched to an absurd degree.

Don't rush an answer – ponder and wonder

The world wants to rush people towards the quickest answer. Yet the best answers come slowly. Taking time to wonder, consider, ponder and dream is almost revolutionary but it's taking that time that allows imagination to build.

We often think of imagination as the ability to visualise things in the external world. Imagination requires accessing inner awareness that is then used to form insights and images.

Give time for the imagination to roam

Boredom is a call to action. Try to resist the temptation to solve boredom for your children. Instead, ask them for several other things they think they could be doing.

Free play expands imagination. Whether it is exploring the natural world or tinkering away inside at a project, play is the building block of creativity and imagination. Some kids stop playing. Some families are so busy they haven't had much time for play. The suggestions below are especially important if you feel you haven't been able to create enough play time in your home.

Non-screen time

We need some time of the day when there are no screens. This applies to us as well as our children. Switching off the computer and putting the phone away says to kids, 'You are the most important person right now'.

Have a creativity corner in your house

If children are not given the space to make creative decisions on their own they won't develop this part of their genius. Children need time, the freedom of choice and the chance to experiment without feeling like they have to produce anything meaningful.

Stock your creativity corner at home with corks, crayons, pieces of felt, glue, sparkles, paints, pipe cleaners, string, beads, coloured paper and collage materials.

Keep a board above the corner with interesting pictures, quotes and ideas. Nearby have a dressing-up box stuffed with old clothes, hats, stuffed animals and puppets.

Put an old mat that can be easily washed or thrown out near the creativity corner. Do not have carpet that cannot be marked or stained.

Give kids space to invent

To be creative kids need to get dirty. Expect mess. Genius does not come in neat packages.

Take your children on creative expeditions. Zoos, museums and aquariums are preferable to toy stores (and probably cheaper in the long term).

Visit farms or plant a garden. Build scrapbooks and photo albums.

Encourage kite building, soapbox car making, model airplanes and photography.

Expose them to many art forms from drawing to playing music to writing, pottery, puppet making, papier mâché and clay modelling. One of the great delights of being a parent is that you get to play as well.

Don't be one of those parents who has parties for their children where everyone gets a prize for everything. Instead, have birthday parties where kids construct or make things. Have cooking challenges, trail-making, weird costume making or playhouse building.

It's great for parents to lead creative ventures, but it's also important to step back as well. You can't help children grow into creative people if you do all the creating yourself. It is hard to be freely creative if you feel someone is watching your every move. If we hover too close we squeeze out our children's creativity.

It takes some bravery for parents not to pressure their children towards improved outcomes. If we step back and watch we can see how our children are doing, not just how well they are doing.

As parents we have a responsibility to model imperfection, especially if we are adept in an area that interests our child. In every creative life there are setbacks.

Look for simple, elegant solutions
Occam's razor is the idea that we should always aim for the simplest solution possible.

The North American Space Agency (NASA) was concerned about astronauts writing in space when they discovered pens did not work well in zero gravity. To overcome this problem, they gathered teams of mechanical, hydrodynamic and chemical engineers and spent millions of dollars developing the space pen. It was a technological marvel. It worked in space, underwater and could write upside down.

The Soviets solved the problem as well. They gave their astronauts pencils.

Teaching children to think SPARKLING creative thoughts

In order to help our children develop their creative genius, we use the acronym **SPARKLING**.

Store good ideas

Pattern detection

Analyse the issue

Reflect and reshape ideas

Kite-flying

Let go

Improvisation and ingenuity

New ways of describing

Grab it and use it

Store good ideas
Find an idea-capturing device. People used to collect and keep bits of string, wire, wool and odd bits and ends that could come in handy for a 'rainy day'. You can collect ideas like this. Keep them on a laptop or a whiteboard, in a notebook or a sketchbook or a drawer

somewhere. Lots of people have lots of good ideas but let them slip away to be forgotten. Geniuses capture their good ideas.

Train yourself and your children to capture good ideas somehow. It's estimated that we have at least twelve inspirational insights every day. That's 84 great ideas you will have collected each week that previously went missing.

Don't be too selective. If an idea seems a bit strange and wonky keep it somewhere. You'll be surprised how often a weird idea comes in handy at unexpected moments. Aim to collect lots of ideas rather than just the seemingly sensible ones. Social media, especially Twitter, is a great way of crowdsourcing lots of ideas about topics.

> *Nothing is more dangerous than an idea when it's the only one you have.*
>
> Emile Chartier

*P*attern detection

Sherlock Holmes the fictional detective said, 'When you have eliminated the impossible, whatever remains, *however improbable,* must be the truth.' Patterns are a series of signs or clues that give you ideas. Noticing patterns involves being observant.

All of us can become more observant. One way to do this it to pick someone and try to notice their mood, body language, the tone of their voice and their facial expressions. You'll be amazed at how much you learn by listening, looking, noticing and observing.

The art of observing the world around you is a rare skill. Be prepared to ask the question 'why' a lot. Notice potential problems and consider solutions. For example, people spend a lot of time staring down at their phones. Will they get sore necks eventually? Will there be more need for osteopaths? Supermarket car parks are often not level. Trolleys have hard metallic edges. Should they have bumpers so they don't scratch cars? If the climate becomes hotter and wetter, will people need more umbrellas? Will they also need more weatherproof boots? Should we invent some rubber boots that don't make your feet hot? We could go on with this but you get the point.

*A*nalyse the issue

George Ainsworth Land, the author of *Grow or Die*, gave five-year-olds a creativity test and found that 98 per cent scored in the highly creative range. When the same children were retested at 10 years of age only 30 per cent were still highly creative and by 15 years just 12 per cent. By adulthood it drops to 2 per cent.

At 5 years of age we ask 65 questions a day. The rate drops to 6 questions at age 44. Our laughter rate also drops from 113 times a day as a child to 11 times a day in adulthood. So adults are less fun and less inquisitive.

Keep your curiosity. Be prepared to sit with a problem or issue without knowing the answer. The fastest way to kill off creativity is to put yourself or your child under pressure to produce a solution within a time frame.

Most great creations are developed over time, like Picasso's famous painting *Guernica*, which he worked and reworked as he painted it.

*R*eflect and reshape ideas

Our world has little time for reflection. Pausing to weigh up and consider the meaning of events or ideas is quickly dismissed. Reflection is often confused with indecision or hesitation.

Leonardo da Vinci thought it was our second thoughts that are the most valuable. Reflection is indeed the pathway towards creativity.

It takes a lot of patience for a restless child or a goal-focused adult to sit patiently without an answer long enough for creativity to emerge. But the best way to distract ourselves while we are waiting for our best ideas to show up is to reshape our ideas.

Start by asking children questions like, 'What if it was smaller/ later/ longer/ closer/ hotter/ colder?' Play with ideas. Be nice to them. Don't torture them into submission. Practise open receptiveness.

Develop an analogy or a metaphor for a problem and pose them to children. For example, is a shopping centre like a beehive? Is blood flowing in the human body like water in plumbing? Are the electrons moving around the nucleus of an atom like planets revolving around the sun?

Stretch the ideas. Try various combinations. Toss them around with your children. Don't stop at the first ideas they have – keep jumbling them around.

Reshaping ideas means looking beyond the limitations of a current situation. Sometimes it involves asking, 'What if the reverse were true?'

The aim is to create multiple descriptions of ideas and concepts that can be used flexibly such as diagrams, outlines, storyboards, cartoons and hierarchies. Edward de Bono's thinking hats can also help achieve this.

*K*ite-flying

Creativity often occurs in the context of soft-focused thinking when people daydream and allow their minds to roam – soar like a kite.

Wolfgang Mozart once commented: 'I can't make the music come. It comes to me and through me ... it comes like a morsel; the music begins to write itself.'

Michael Jackson also once said that the music came to him in dreams. Keith Richards also describes hearing the now famous riff for the song 'Satisfaction' in a dream and leaping out of bed to write it down.

Let go

Whether or not Archimedes really did get inspiration while taking a bath, the story makes an important point. Your brain is more than capable of working on problems while you loaf off. Switch off. Let it simmer. Sleep on it. Sleep reorganises our thinking.

The creation of routines for children can support the development of creativity. Creativity occurs when we slow down. It requires exposure to a broad range of experiences and then using them to improvise and innovate. Resilient learners go beyond accurately perceiving events and obstacles around them to developing creative ways to utilise these experiences.

Improvisation and ingenuity

Creativity is a bit like making a fire – sometimes you get a bright spark but mostly it's about huffing and puffing. The more you can give children the routines within which to learn efficiently and the chance to deliberate and reflect over problems that challenge and interest them, the more likely you are to develop resilient learners.

Ingenuity means thinking about how things can be used in different situations. Asking your child, 'What else is this like?' and 'How could I use this in other situations?' builds mindfulness, awareness and flexible thinking.

Feed your child's brain with great ideas. Look around for examples of people who have come up with inventive creative ideas to use as role models and build upon. Sometimes it helps to gain ideas from different areas of thinking. When Mercedes-Benz wanted to develop a new small car they didn't look at other car designers. They consulted Swatch, the makers of watches. Together they developed the Smart Car.

Improvisation is about transfer of knowledge. It involves asking yourself, 'How else or where else could I use this?' You can encourage your child by just asking this question.

Obviously great jazz musicians and great chefs are improvisers. Improvisational thinking can lead to great success. The person who thought about wheels and suitcases and put the two together to create the roller case was really onto something. The person who tasted an avocado and thought, 'You know, this could taste pretty good with a few prawns on top,' was also on a winner. Improvisational thinking and transfer occur when we look beyond the surface characteristics of situations and problems to see what features they have in common.

Always consider how an idea could be useful in another setting. A drug company released a medication called minoxidil that lowered blood pressure. Although it was effective for this, it had one important side effect. It stimulated hair growth. So while it was used a bit by people wanting to lower their blood pressure, it was mainly used by balding men to regrow their hair.

A manufacturer made a machine for spraying crops in cold climates. Unfortunately it didn't work. The spray froze and killed the crops. Another person looked at the machine and used it to make snow on ski slopes and made a fortune.

One way you can develop the flexible thinking that underlies ingenuity and improvisation is to have your child draw things from different perspectives. Put something on the floor then ask your child to stand on a chair and draw the object from above. Then draw it from underneath. Ask them to imagine you are drawing a city from the perspective of a bird or while hovering in a helicopter, or draw a pond from the perspective of a fish.

Another activity that is fun for families to play that can help children think about different perspectives is to create a story based on the roll of a dice. Each number refers to a different element of the story, as seen on the next page.

The roll-a-dice story creator				
1. Type of Story	2. Emotional Content	3. Context	4. Setting	5. Your Personality
1. Western	Love	Adversity	A sinking ship	Nervous
2.Romance	Hate	Opportunity	A haunted house	Depressed
3. Horror	Betrayal	Loving support	A party	Murderous
4. Comedy	Desire	Conflict	A cinema	Shifty
5. Adventure	Greed	Envy	A hot air balloon	Romantic
6. Drama	Surprise	Ruthless cunning	A runaway train	Gushy

To play, someone rolls the dice once to work out the type of story you are going to create. Roll again for the emotional content and setting of the story. Each person rolls the dice to determine their personality in the story. Use your imagination to create a story either individually or together.

New ways of describing

The creative mind is a lot like many ping pong balls rumbling around in a lottery basket. You are never quite sure which ideas or balls are going to come out and in which sequence.

If you take a box of Lego pieces and rattle it about a bit it is like a child's mind, combining and reconnecting ideas.

Ask children to find the second right answer. Leonardo da Vinci believed the first way he looked at a problem was too biased towards his usual ways of seeing things. Plato said it is better to answer one question eight different ways than eight different questions one way.

Another family dice-based game to encourge flexible thinking is the roll-a-dice vehicle designer. A similar activity can be done with parents and children to increase flexibility of thinking. In this activity, again use a dice to determine the features of a vehicle children design.

Players roll a dice to find out what medium the vehicle has to travel over, roll again for the source of power and again for the purpose of the vehicle. Then have your child design such a vehicle.

The roll-a-dice vehicle designer		
Medium it travels over	Source of power	Purpose
1. Air	1. Petrol	1. Sports
2. Water	2. Nuclear power	2. Military
3. Land	3. Methane gas	3. Exploration
4. Outer Space	4. Jet propulsion	4. Personal Transport
5. Mountains	5. Horse drawn	5. Romance
6. Underwater	6. Steam	6. Moving animals

Fun will no doubt result from watching your child work out how to design a romantic horse-drawn vehicle that travels through outer space while you design a methane-powered romantic vehicle that travels across water.

Grab it and use it

> *Some people see things as they are and say why? I dream*
> *things that never were and say, why not?*
>
> Robert F Kennedy adapting the words of George Bernard Shaw

Encourage your children to always capture their thoughts in some way. Not having a method for capturing insightful ideas is like having a pond full of fish but no way to fish.

People spend a lot of energy telling you why things can't be done. Ignore them. Just because a problem is solved doesn't mean we should stop thinking creatively about it. When Steve Jobs developed the iPod, he didn't stop there.

Help your children develop creativity and use their imagination by encouraging them to keep asking, 'What would happen if ...?' questions.

Building creativity and imagination	
Ages 2–4	■ Play. ■ Focus on experiences and associations. ■ Use questions as kick-off points for larger enquiries. ■ Search for beauty in the world. ■ Create a fairy garden. ■ Put on a play using sock puppets. ■ Build towns in sand pits with little houses, cars, trees. ■ Make tents inside the house.
Ages 5–7	■ Tell children they are already creative people. ■ Develop their curiosity. ■ Have a creativity corner in your home.

	■ Expect children to get messy and dirty – genius is not always neat. ■ Take children on creative expeditions. ■ Let your children see you being creative. ■ Switch off all electronics and do some projects together such as building a tower out of pipe cleaners. ■ Learn to whistle. ■ Learn to click your fingers. ■ Play the recorder. ■ Learn to tap dance. ■ Write a letter in code. ■ Write a letter with invisible ink. ■ Do magic tricks. ■ Make crystals. ■ Make bracelets. ■ Have 'crafternoons' when children can do craft. ■ Make masks out of papier mâché. ■ Go fishing.
Ages 8–11	■ Expose children to comedy especially shows that include absurd connections between ideas. ■ Discuss some common issues people have and talk about possible imaginative solutions. ■ Encourage improvisational dance, theatre, art and music activities. ■ Help out but also step back and let them invent things of their own. ■ Aim to have children experience making masks, maps, puppets, toys, craft works, tapestry, pottery, music, art works, poems.

	<ul><li>Some children love performance, others do not. Consider if this builds or detracts from creativity.</li><li>Ensure that creativity time is fun time and whatever is produced is not judged, just enjoyed.</li><li>Do judo.</li><li>Make ceramics.</li><li>Go snorkelling.</li><li>Learn circus skills.</li></ul>
Ages 12–18	<ul><li>Acknowledge inventiveness and creativity.</li><li>Visit art galleries, music performances and festivals, theatre, films and opera.</li><li>Encourage writing songs and poems, completing art pieces, junk sculptures.</li><li>Play improvisational and experimental music.</li><li>Engage in improv theatre games.</li><li>Write a comic book and do cartooning.</li><li>Design and make a sculpture.</li><li>Learn about marine biology.</li><li>Go to comedy shows or write jokes.</li><li>Do some Dada art.</li></ul>

Chapter 11

Organising information

There is a brilliant child locked inside every student.

Marva Collins

Think of your child's mind as if it were a wardrobe. Most people have things scattered all over the place. The socks are jumbled up with the shirts and the coat that should hang on the hook has gone missing. Ideas and knowledge can get jumbled in much the same way.

Geniuses don't waste time. They organise what they know so that it can be retrieved when needed, linked to other things where possible and used regularly.

We live in an age of infoglut. Most people are swamped with information and become overwhelmed. The Rex part of the brain – the part that really doesn't want to work too hard and just wants to get back to resting and surviving – becomes distracted or irritated. This turns bright kids into passive recipients rather than producers of knowledge.

The way we organise information inside our heads affects our ability to focus, store and retrieve knowledge. It also influences our creativity – you can't link ideas in new ways if you can't access them easily.

In a cluttered and frenetic world where a thousand things clamour for our attention, we need to help our children and ourselves become discerning recipients of information.

Fill your mind with inspirational thoughts and it will amaze you. Fill your mind with junk and guess what you get? This means trying to expose your child to the very best ideas, books, movies, pieces of music and activities.

Ten ways to declutter your child's mind

1. Have a day a week when you minimise your whole family's exposure to electronic media.
2. Have at least one family meal (many more if you can) without electronic distractions.
3. Use your router or airport system to prevent access to the internet after a set hour each night.
4. Firmly discourage checking social media sites during conversations. When you are with people be with them. Practise being present.
5. Try to have conversations about ideas as well as events. Rather than always asking children how their day was, ask them what their big idea or thought of the day was.
6. Know that news services take a proctological view of life. They report the most sensational and negative stories. Be wary of watching the news: some children find it distressing and become preoccupied with it.
7. Avoid commercial advertising wherever possible.
8. Know that anxiety can cause children to think in repetitive loops where they ruminate. Talk with them about the options and use the decision-making model PICCA (see Chapter 7) to lead them towards action.
9. Do activities with your children that require them to be in the moment. For example, it is difficult to catch a ball, shoot for goal, juggle, surf or ski if you are thinking about other things.
10. If you have read a story or seen a film, have conversations about what they think was the main idea or most important message.

Help children learn things in the way they will most likely use them

If I asked you to tell me the months of the year, you would list them fairly easily. If, however, I asked you to tell me the months of the year in alphabetical order you might struggle a bit more.

The point here is to teach your child in precisely the same way that you want them to use the information. If you want them to pack their lunch for school, you might want them to remember to put the ingredients into their lunch box in the order they will eat them. For example, snack for break, sandwiches for lunch, fruit, a drink.

Ladders of understanding and the art of backwards learning

One of the best ways to learn something new is to learn it backwards. Backwards learning uses ladders of understanding and is a very powerful way of organising knowledge. I suspect you already have used this process even if you've never heard of ladders of understanding because this is precisely the way most people learn to tie their shoelaces.

Do you remember how you learned this skill? It is probable that someone made two loops for you and asked you to tie them together. Once you could tie the loops, they then asked you to form one loop. Then the other loop. Eventually, you can complete the whole task by learning each step in backwards order.

Very cleverly the person teaching you gave you a sense of mastery (tying your own shoelaces) before teaching the steps you needed to be able to get that sense of mastery.

This is also why children often learn to brush or dry the dog after a bath before being given the task of washing the dog.

The application of ladders of understanding goes well beyond tying shoelaces and washing dogs. The same method can be used to help children learn procedures, processes and ways to solve problems.

For example, let's say I have a five-step procedure such as solving a maths problem or completing an essay. We might outline the steps involved as follows.

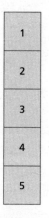

Then we might develop a similar five-step procedure and outline the first four steps and ask the child to complete the fifth.

| 1 |
| 2 |
| 3 |
| 4 |
| ? |

This then continues with several parallel problems.

1	1	1	1	1	?
2	2	2	2	?	?
3	3	3	?	?	?
4	4	?	?	?	?
5	?	?	?	?	?

As you can see, the child is given all five steps at first and then in a parallel example the first four and they have to work out the last step, then the first three, then the last two and so on.

Ladders of understanding help children to see there are sequences in activities like writing a good essay, learning to play a musical piece, completing a scientific experiment or solving a maths problem.

Outlining the steps involved in solving a problem also helps children develop self-explanations where they can think to themselves, 'First I've got to do this and then I've got to ...'

Children who can think through and explain to themselves the steps involved in solving a problem get better results at school, especially in science subjects.

Ladders of understanding outline problems using the same structure, helping children to increase their pattern recognition. Children begin to see that some types of problems are asking you to solve the same issue expressed in different ways. For example:

Problem 1

I had five birds. Three flew away. How many are left?

$5 - 3 = ?$

Problem 2

I had some birds. Three flew away. I now have two. How many did I start with?

$? - 3 = 2$

Problem 3

I had five birds. Some flew away. I have two left. How many flew away?

$5 - ? = 2$

Problem 4

I had some birds and some flew away. I now have two left.

What number of birds might I have started with?

How many might have flown away?

How many different combinations can you find?

Is there a pattern?

Grouping and categorising

From an early age children can learn to group objects in different ways, such as shape, size, colour and texture. They can also learn to associate concepts with categories. For example, which of the following do we associate with winter: sunscreen, snow, frost, football, blossoms, hot days or fireplaces?

Once children have got the skills of associating concepts with a category, they can move to comparing two or more categories using Venn diagrams.

To help children learn about Venn diagrams, take two (or more) concepts and consider how they are different and how they overlap. For example, dogs and giraffes both have four legs, breathe, eat and run about, but only dogs bark, wag their tails and gnaw on bones and only giraffes have long necks and are mainly found in Africa.

The easiest way to illustrate this for children is to place some hoops on the ground then put ideas or pictures on pieces of paper and sort them into the different sections. You can then ask children to duplicate this Venn diagram they have made on paper, discussing it with you as they go.

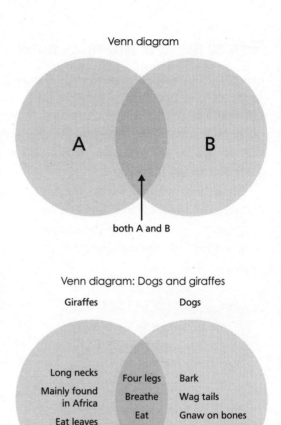

Venn diagram

both A and B

Venn diagram: Dogs and giraffes

Giraffes — Dogs

Long necks / Mainly found in Africa / Eat leaves from trees | Four legs / Breathe / Eat / Run | Bark / Wag tails / Gnaw on bones / May chase balls

Why this is so important for children to learn is because we know that identifying similarities and differences results in a 45 percentile point improvement in school marks.

How to make memorable notes

One of the best ways to organise information is to create notes. Most geniuses have intricate systems of filing, storing and organising information. Their system may look haphazard to the casual observer but it is there. Geniuses methodically and systematically capture good ideas related to their interests and organise them in ways that are useful to them.

From 2001 onwards with teachers from around the world, I conducted 'practical intelligence projects' looking for some of the more powerful ways to help children learn. The note system outlined here evolved from those discussions.

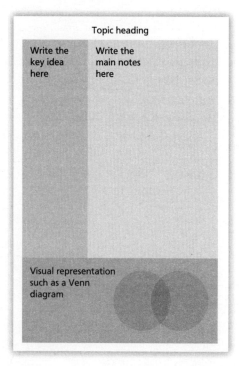

Essentially it is an adaptation of the Cornell method of note-making and involves children writing a heading for the topic at the top of the page and then dividing it into three main sections.

1 In the largest one children write their main notes.

2 In the sidebar they write the most important bits of information or the key ideas.

3 At the bottom they convert the same knowledge into a visual. A Venn diagram is ideal but a bubble or concept map can also work.

With younger children, it can be useful if you take them through developing a set of notes on a book they have read. Playing games such as identifying the main point of a film, story or TV show helps children learn to pick out the key ideas.

In an overloaded, distracted world, a person who knows how to focus on the most important piece of information, pick out the key idea, and identify the crux of something is at a major advantage.

By using this note-making system, they have transformed the same bit of knowledge into three different formats: main notes, key idea and a visual representation, and increased the retention of that knowledge.

The problem is it takes human beings 24 repetitions of anything to get to 80 per cent of competence. How do you get kids to repeat anything 24 times? Next I'll show you how to give their memory a hand.

Giving memory a hand – a repetition method
Once children have learned something, ask them to summarise it by making a summary hand.

Have them cut out cardboard shapes of their hand. (Very young children may need you to cut it out for them.) Then ask children to give their memory a hand.

On one side of the cardboard hand they write the five most important pieces of knowledge about a topic – one on each finger or thumb. Some examples might be:

Five features of autumn: changing leaves, temperature drop, rain, cooling soil, shorter days.

Five phases of art history: renaissance, neoclassicism, romanticism, modern, contemporary.

Five types of chemical reactions: combustion, synthesis, decomposition, acid-based, single and double displacement.

In the palm area they either draw a Venn diagram or write a more detailed summary of the topic in point form.

They then turn their summary hand over and write:

- their name
- two questions that they can use to test their memory of the topic
- one question that is really tricky.

They then assign a point value to the tricky question.

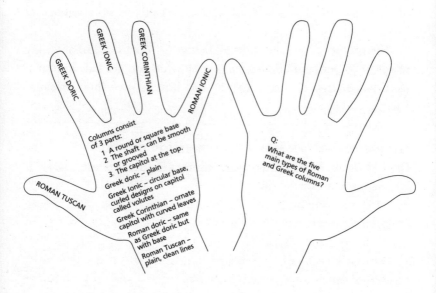

Be patient! It will take children time to develop the skill of making a good summary hand to organise information. Ideally you will help them to learn this skill over several years.

This method has been used successfully with children of all ages, substantially decreasing the number of repetitions children need to understand key concepts. It helps secondary school students organise and revise main ideas and prepare for exams. It helps younger kids organise their thoughts.

Every so often, have children test their memory and knowledge by trying to answer the questions before turning over the hand to check the answer.

> *I choose a block of marble and chop off whatever I don't need.*
>
> Auguste Rodin (1840–1917)
> when asked how he managed to make his remarkable statues.

Help children develop notes with flair and memorability

Teaching children ways to take down and organise the information they learn provides a powerful way of increasing their memory.

The last thing kids want is a set of boring notes. So help them to develop colourful notes with attention-grabbing elements.

Use varying sizes so that some words **STAND OUT!**

Some children become anxious at school and want to write everything down. Teach them to use symbols and abbreviations.

Teaching children organisation skills	
Ages 2–4	<ul><li>Start using ladders of understanding with different colours for different family procedures such as getting up in the morning, getting ready for bed.</li><li>Have times when exposure to electronic media is minimised and keep this going over the years.</li><li>Highlight and discuss similarities between things then discuss differences.</li></ul>

Ages 5–7	■ Use ladders of understanding to teach basic skills – how to write a story, how to tie your shoelaces, how to solve a problem. ■ Use hula hoops to sort out differences and similarities as a way of introducing Venn diagrams. ■ Do simple science experiments. ■ Try out basic chemistry sets. ■ Use microscopes and make a record of observations. ■ Build playhouses. ■ Play the xylophone.
Ages 8–11	■ Use ladders of understanding to teach how to make a decision. ■ Play games where children try to work out the main point or message of a story, TV show, film or picture book. ■ Teach children how to make notes. If your child's teacher is using a different method share this book with them. ■ Make 'hands' to summarise main points. ■ Do basic carpentry. ■ Construct soapbox cars. ■ Play cello, violin, piano, guitar. ■ Play forensics games. ■ Do brain puzzles. ■ Fix a punctured bicycle tyre. ■ Use Betty Edwards' *Drawing on the Right Side of the Brain* to develop observation and artistic skills. ■ Do thinking puzzles. ■ Plan dinners, meals, shopping trips, holidays, birthday parties and weekly schedules.

Ages 12–18	<ul><li>As some teenagers mistakenly believe they have grown beyond all of that, re-teach them how to make notes.</li><li>Encourage them to make wildly interesting notes.</li><li>Do not be convinced when they say, 'I can take a photo of the board with my phone' or 'I'll remember it'. Handwritten notes are much more powerful.</li><li>Use Venn diagrams to help them to clarify their thinking.</li><li>Remind them about creating charts like the ones covered in Chapter 6 on planning.</li><li>Teach them how to create summary hands and use them when revising for tests and exams (covered in the next chapter).</li><li>Take them trekking, hiking and camping.</li><li>Engage them in devil's advocate debates.</li><li>Give them mind puzzles to do.</li><li>Teach them basic mechanics.</li><li>Learn how to validate information accessed online by investigating hoaxes and phishing.</li></ul>

CHAPTER 12

Improving memory and learning

I've had amnesia for as long as I can remember.

Steve Wright, stand-up comedian

Rattling off pi to 50 decimal places or calculating vast sums in your head are things most of us can't do. And being able to recall the exact sequence of cards being played would probably get you banned from most of the world's casinos, hopefully after you'd made a lot of cash. But many of us don't try to remember things any more as we have enormous amounts of information literally at our fingertips. Just as the calculator has been described as the great leveller, the internet is the greatest library ever known to humanity.

However, memory correlates highly with intelligence, and increasing your child's memory is one of the most powerful things a parent can do to unlock a child's genius.

Children who use successful strategies for remembering information will find it easier to learn, study and take exams. School requires more memory skills than any job you can think of. Writing, spelling, maths and taking tests are the school activities that require the most memory, but unfortunately very few schools give their students memory-training skills.

Along with helping kids to concentrate, improving their memory is probably the most sure-fire way of increasing school marks. Just as we saw with motivation, helping them learn a few basic strategies can increase children's memory and performance.

Sleeping on it

What you do just before you go to sleep is what you remember best. Anything you read or study just before sleep is processed in your dreams and your dreams are where your memories consolidate.

When I work with actors learning scripts for movies or plays I have them listen to audio recordings of themselves reading their part just before they go to sleep. When I work with students who want to achieve high levels at school, we use exactly the same strategy. Listening to an audio recording of the main points you wish to remember just before you go to sleep greatly increases your chances of recalling it.

In schools I get groups of students to create audio recordings of key topic areas using different voices. This way they are not only able to revise their knowledge just before they sleep, they can also pair key concepts with a particular person's voice.

This means children shouldn't study, phone a friend and then sleep. To foster optimal consolidation the order should be phone call, study then sleep.

This is why it is always good to remind your children that you love them before they go to sleep and why you should try to never go to sleep on an argument with your partner.

Having additional glucose

Having additional glucose 20 minutes before a test or an assessment task increases memory. As long as it is medically safe for your child to have additional glucose, you may wish to try this out by purchasing some glucose tablets. A couple of jelly beans also works.

Stimulating the vagus nerve

Another tip for enhancing memory is to stimulate the vagus nerve, a cranial nerve that links our brain stem with our abdomen and many organs in between. My Chinese medical colleagues have informed me that an acupressure point for the vagus nerve is in the indentation at the back of your neck. Rubbing the back of your neck stimulates the nerve. Another way of stimulating it is by taking deep breaths, which also helps in relaxing! Try it for yourself when you want to remember something.

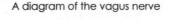

A diagram of the vagus nerve

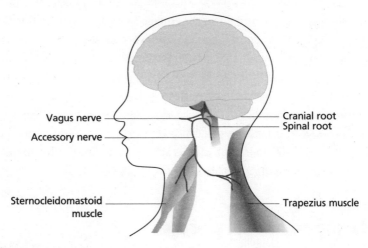

Making it visual

Children remember visuals more than words or sounds. When helping them learn or understand something new add a picture, flow chart, map, drawing or outline whenever you can.

Learning in 20-minute bursts

Generally, if we are trying to remember a list of things we'll recall the first few and the last few items and be most likely to forget the middle ones. The same rule applies to learning periods, class time and homework time.

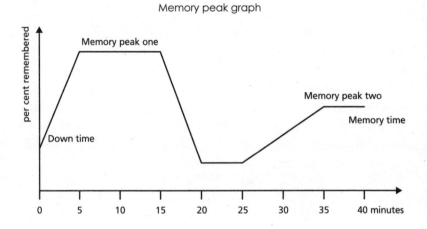

Memory peak graph

My research with many schools shows that children's eyes start to glaze over and their memory goes to mush after about 20 minutes. Consequently, teachers often divide longer lesson times into 20-minute phases.

This means that short bursts of 20 minutes of memory time may work best at home. So dragging homework on for endless hours may not be as effective as either doing it in 20-minute bursts or at least changing the study subject every 20 minutes or so.

To maximise memory in a learning experience, change tack every 20 minutes or so. For example, you might read to your child for 20 minutes (depending of course on the age and interest of your child) then talk about the story or have a chat about other ideas related to the story.

Being actively involved

> *I hear and I forget.*
> *I see and I remember.*
> *I do and I understand.*

Confucius, Chinese philosopher and reformer (551BC–479BC).

The more actively your children are involved in something the more likely they are to remember it.

From the pyramid of memory below, you can see that this means that you will only remember 10 per cent of what you have read in this book tomorrow! However, if you then talk about it with someone else, your memory jumps to 50 per cent and if you decide to actually use this information to help your child, your memory leaps to 90 per cent.

The pyramid of memory

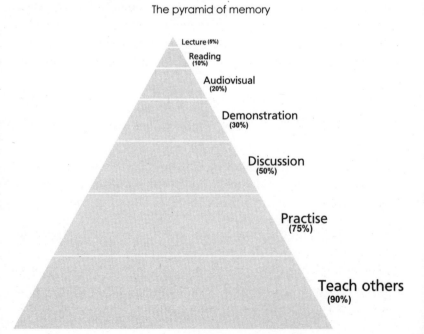

One way to learn something new would be to hear it, then create a diagram about it, practise it, see if it works, hear some more about it until you get it right, then tell or teach someone else what you have learned.

The pyramid of memory also shows you that what you do and the way that you do it will be more likely to be recalled by children than the words that you use.

This is why it is so important for parents of young geniuses to live their lives well. To show their children that life can be adventurous, learning can be fun, that success is worth striving for and that being an adult can be enjoyable!

The man who remembered everyone: the BASE method

It was a hard crowd to impress at Billy Reed's Little Club on East 55th Street, New York in the 1940s, but Harry Lorayne, memory specialist extraordinaire, managed it. Harry's method was to meet all the people in the audience and get to know their name. Harry would then open his show by asking all the people he met to please stand up. He'd ask them to sit down as he pointed to each person and said his or her name.

Harry used a number of methods but the main one he developed was the BASE method. **BASE** stands for:

Big
Active
Substitute
Exaggerate

When using the BASE method to remember something you should imagine it as big and active, substitute it and exaggerate.

For example, let's say you wanted to remember to take some fish home with you from work. You might make a picture in your mind of yourself driving home with a gigantic fish sitting beside you and thousands of little fish flapping around in the back seat. Or if you wanted to remember to take an umbrella when you go out, you could imagine yourself opening the door with a gigantic umbrella.

Lorayne remembered names through auditory associations, which he called the Substitute Word system. Images are related to outstanding features on the person's face to create a composite, absurd image that is easy to remember. The five rules of using this system to remember names are:

1   Listen clearly to the name.
2   Try to spell the name in your head.
3   Make a remark about the name.
4   Use the name during your initial conversation.
5   Say the name when you say goodbye and relate it to an outstanding feature on the person's face.

Surnames in the Lorayne system are classed into three categories of meaning:

- Names with obvious or inherent meaning (Bowman, Swan, Abbot, Priestley).
- Names with immediate associational recognition (Versace, Faulkner, Berra).
- Names with no clear association or meaning (Maurello, Baldwin, Akakievich, Bennett).

This last category is linked to similar sounding words. So Bennett would become 'Ben it' or 'Bin it' and Baldwin could be turned into 'bald one' or 'bald win'.

I know it sounds a bit weird but it works!

BASE is a good strategy for making things more memorable. If you learn even a few of Harry's methods and hand them on to your child you will sow the seeds of success for them.

Methods for improving the different types of memory

There are basically three main types of memory: immediate memory, working memory and long-term memory.

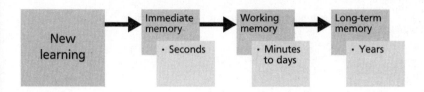

Immediate memory

This part of our memory only last five seconds and unless we use the information quickly we discard it from awareness.

The amount of information that people can hold in their immediate memory is very consistent. The golden rule of human memory is that people can usually remember between five and nine pieces of information at any one time.

For young children under five years of age, the amount that can be held in immediate memory is less – between one and three bits of information. In fact a good rule of thumb to remember when asking your child to do something is 'age plus one': the number of words in an instruction should only equal their age plus one.

So if you said, 'Please finish your drink of milk and brush your teeth because we will be late to school' (17 words) to most six-year-olds, they would be well entitled to look blankly at you and say, 'Huh?' Break it down. One instruction at a time.

If the number of things we can keep in our immediate memory is seven you might be thinking, 'Okay, wise guy, if that's so, how come most phone numbers are at least eight numbers long and we can remember them?' Well, the answer is that we learn to chunk or break pieces of information down into smaller bits, so rather than remembering a phone number as 0209491328 we learn to break it down to 020-949-1328.

Breaking it down also helps us to remember strings of letters. For example, if I asked you to remember this series of letters, most people would have some difficulty.

F D R B B C C I A E U F B I U K J F K N Y C U S A

But if we break it down in some way that is even slightly meaningful it becomes much easier to remember.

F D R
B B C
C I A
E U
F B I
U K
J F K
N Y C
U S A

Breaking it down for children means delivering important instructions in bite-sized chunks. For example, ask children to find Africa on a map. Now see if they can locate Kenya. Now see if they can work out the capital of Kenya (Nairobi).

Working memory

Working memory is where you hold information that is likely to be needed when you haven't really decided whether you want to keep it forever. This is where ideas are combined and developed. Every time you go shopping you use your working memory to recall what you need or want. The most powerful way to build working memory is interest.

Children can usually hold something in their working memory for five to ten minutes. For teenagers, it's often ten to fifteen minutes. For the retention to continue, there needs to be some change in the way the information is used or other connections made. This is where paraphrasing skills become so important.

Paraphrasing

The way we all remember key bits of information is to break it down into simpler messages. Paraphrasing involves picking the key ideas in any message.

You can help your children to develop the skills of paraphrasing. Ask them to give you summaries of stories, TV shows and films.

You can also ask children to summarise an article in 100 words, then create a summary of the summary in 50 words, 25 words and so on. You can also play games like 'in ten words or less, tell me the main bits of a story'.

Long-term memory

Long-term memory is where we keep the serious stuff that we really need to know. When something goes into long-term memory it becomes processed by different parts of the brain. That seems to free us up to be able to concentrate on other things.

Having information in your long-term memory not only allows you to remember who your friends and family are when you wake up in the morning it also means you don't always have to learn things from scratch.

There are a couple of important things to know about how long-term memory works.

1 **The best way to put information into long-term memory is not just to read it over and over again.** Just reading over your notes is not a good way of preparing for exams. The best way to

remember information is to transform it by putting words into pictures, or pictures into words or sounds.

2   **The way we put information into long-term memory is different from the way we get it out again.** Information gets stored in long-term memory on the basis of its similarity to other pieces of information. The way that we *get* information *out* again is based on difference.

For example, let's say when you were a child your family got you a pet dog. You learned and remembered that you had a pet dog by learning about the similarities to other dogs – four legs, furry, barks and so on. Let's imagine that *your* dog was lost and you had to go to the dog pound to find it. You would draw on the image in your head of what your dog looks like to find it. Using similarities wouldn't help much in trying to find your dog: 'Mmm … let's see … it has four legs, barks a bit, gets smelly' – that wouldn't help you much. So you would use critical distinctive aspects of your dog to find it: 'Mmm … let's see … it has a spot on its left shoulder and a kink in its tail'. We remember ideas in just the same way – same, same but different.

This means when we want to learn something and remember it we need to recognise how it is similar to other things and in what ways it is different from others.

3   **Getting something stored into long-term memory takes time.** After learning something new the brain needs several hours to consolidate it. For students in higher education this is vital information because long-term filing works best if you go right to sleep. The minutes before bedtime are crucial (see the section 'Sleep on it' earlier in this chapter).

The best way to remember something is to transform it. If it's visual, put it into words. If it's verbal, create a picture or graph of it. Use lists, acronyms, tables and graphics and link new information to prior learning. This is why high-performing students don't just do homework they also spend some time each week reorganising their notes so that they are memorable.

Following are some other methods to improve how your brain stores long-term memories.

The journey method

Leonardo Da Vinci used a long-term memory enhancement strategy known as the journey method. Let's say you need to remember ten things. To recall them you think of a journey that you know so well that your children could do it almost with their eyes closed. It might be the journey from their bedroom to the toilet and back again. It only matters that they know the journey very, very well.

Then ask them to select ten landmarks along the journey and start to pair the ten things they want to remember with the landmarks – one thing they want to remember paired with each landmark. Later when they need to recall the items they think of their journey.

For example, if you had to remember ten Greek philosophers you might associate each one with a feature of the landscape between your house and the shops.

Landscape marker	Information to be remembered
1. Go out front gate	Aristotle
2. Turn left	Cleomenes
3. Pass the pine tree	Diogenes
4. Pass the bus stop	Epictetus
5. Turn right	Epicurus
6. Cross the road	Plato
7. Turn left	Plutarch
8. Walk past the bakery	Pythagoras
9. Pass the bike stand	Socrates
10. Enter the shop	Thales

Another way of doing this is to use ten memorable moments in your life. For example, when I was one years old I was given a teddy bear and I can picture Aristotle holding the bear.

The peg method

Another memory strategy is the peg method. This method teaches children ten 'pegs' or words associated with numbers, that they can use to recall anything. (Some children find the peg method really helpful, others just get confused. Test it out.) They do this by pairing the piece of information with each peg. The pegs need to be taught to kids so well that they know them backwards.

The problem with many pegs is that they are a bit too polite to be remembered. So depending on your preference as a parent (and the age of your children) below are two sets of pegs – one polite, one not so polite.

	Polite peg	Not-so-polite peg	Example
One	Sun	Bum	Aristotle
Two	Shoe	Poo	Cleomenes
Three	Flea	Wee	Diogenes
Four	Paw	Gore	Epictetus
Five	Jive	Jive	Epicurus
Six	Sticks	Sick	Plato
Seven	Heaven	Heaven	Plutarch
Eight	Ate	Ate	Pythagoras
Nine	Shine	Shine	Socrates
Ten	Hen	Hen	Thales

In this example you would pair Aristotle with the sun by perhaps imagining an old man called Aristotle sitting in the sunshine, while nearby Epicurus is jiving and Thales is holding a hen.

Make up acronyms

Acronyms are words or sentences in which each letter signifies a different piece of information. The sentence 'My Very Educated Mother Just Sent Us Nine Pizzas' helps people to remember the planets in relation to the sun with the first letter of each word signifying a planet. Another example is 'Every Good Boy Deserves Fruit' which helps people to remember the lines of the music staff. 'Eddie Ate Dynamite Good Bye Eddie' helps guitarists learn the notes of each string (EADGBE).

Acronyms can be based on anything your child is interested in – motorbikes, musicians, dinosaurs or film stars' names.

Medical students use the acronym PEST OF 6 to recall the cranial bones. Each letter stands for a cranial bone, and the number 6 reminds you that there are six of them.

P: Parietal bone
E: Ethmoid bone
S: Sphenoid bone
T: Temporal bone
O: Occipital bone
F: Frontal bone

Chemistry students recall the first 11 elements of the periodic table by recounting:

Harry	He	Likes	Beer	By	Cupfuls	Not	Over	Flowing
Hydrogen	Helium	Lithium	Beryllium	Boron	Carbon	Nitrogen	Oxygen	Fluorine

Make it meaningful

The golden rule for enhancing long-term memory is make it meaningful!

Help your children bolster their memory by underlining or highlighting words. Show them how to go back over learned information and summarise it. Then ask them to create summary hands with questions on one side and answers on the other to test themselves (see Chapter 12). Some high-performing students make an audio recording of things they need to remember for each subject and play it to themselves.

You can also help children improve their memory by practising recalling information under different conditions. If your child stresses out in exams, give him or her practice at remembering under similar conditions.

Helping children perform better in tests and exams

Most people experience some anxiety before a test or exam. Anxiety is partly a result of increased levels of cortisol in the bloodstream. Cortisol can block memory. This is why many people have experienced sitting in an exam feeling like they have forgotten everything they ever learned.

To reduce cortisol children need to learn, study and revise in repetitive, routine ways. Following a system reduces anxiety.

If possible a few days before a test, ask an anxious child to write out their fears on a piece of paper. This helps externalise the fear, and by acknowledging them, the fears often lessen or diminish. Help children to learn that breathing out slowly calms them down, because deep breathing stimulates the vegas nerve (see page 186), and triggers a relaxation response.

If it is possible to find out where they will be sitting in the test room, a few days before the test, get them to sit in the exact position. Just doing this can calm fearful children down.

Throughout the year (and especially in the senior years of school) encourage them to take notes according to the method outlined in Chapter 11. Help them to learn how to pick out the main idea.

Just reading over notes doesn't work. It is boring and can deceive children into believing they know or understand something when they don't. What really embeds knowledge into memory is transforming the information – from notes, to hands, to podcasts – and self-testing. Each week make a summary hand (see Chapter 12). Use different coloured cardboard for different learning areas. Encourage children to use the hands to test themselves on a weekly basis.

Have your children sort the summary hands they get correct into one pile and those they get wrong into another. They should then focus their studies on the ones they answered incorrectly until they get 100 per cent on a re-test. Then recombine the two piles, shuffle and re-test.

Children can then make a podcast based on the hands and combine this with the journey or peg method.

This means that revision doesn't just occur a few weeks before a test or exam, it occurs throughout the year.

A powerful study routine for children
1. Study the entire subject or area of learning.
2. Devise a test to assess whether you understand it.
3. Look at the areas you need to work on.
4. Specifically study those areas.
5. Re-test.
6. Study the entire subject again.
7. Devise another test to assess whether you understood it.
8. Work specifically on the areas you don't understand.

Key words used in exam questions

Term	Meaning
Account for	Give a reason for something.
Analyse	Break a concept down into its component parts, or essential features, in order to examine relationships.
Analysis	An examination and identification of the components of a whole.
Assess	Determine the importance of something.
Calculate	Give a precise answer where there is only one possible answer.
Compare	Describe two situations then present similarities and differences.
Define	Set out the meaning of a term. State precisely the meaning of a concept.
Describe	Give an account of something. An explanation is not required.
Discuss	Consider, or examine. Make a detailed and careful investigation of two sides of an argument.
Distinguish	Make clear an understanding of similar terms.
Evaluate	Determine the significance of something.
Examine	Inspect closely.
Explain	Give the reason for or the cause of something. A description is not sufficient; an explanation of why something has occurred is required.

Illustrate	Show clearly, provide with visual material, and clarify by means of an example.
Outline	Give the important features of the topic.
To what extent?	Give a balanced judgment on a situation where there is some difference of view.
What?	An instruction to make something clearer.
Why?	Give reasons for the existence of something.

Do's and don'ts of writing essays

Do	Don't
Find your strongest point and put it in both the first and last paragraph of the essay.	Bury your best points away in the middle paragraphs.
Answer the question given.	Ignore the key words.
Plan your answer.	Start writing before planning your answer.
Analyse the question.	Give too many ideas away in your first paragraph.
Answer all parts of the question.	List points.
Define all key terms.	Ignore the last parts of the question.
Divide into logically arranged paragraphs.	Use slang, abbreviations, offensive language or text language.
Include an introduction.	
Develop points in full.	

Use labelled diagrams if you can.

Include a conclusion that directly addresses the question.

Use examples and illustrations where appropriate.

Write legibly.

Ensure that each sentence really is a sentence.

Discriminate between relevant and irrelevant points.

Try to summarise everything in your conclusion.

Write in the first person unless asked for a personal account.

Memory games and activities

Ages 2–4	<ul><li>Play memory games to learn the alphabet, read words, remember what to do next, how to pack up, how to get ready. Life is full of opportunities to test and increase memory.</li><li>Start discussions about the main things they know about a subject, eg summer, waterfalls, ducks.</li><li>Play peek-a-boo and hide and seek.</li><li>Practise talking and dialling with a toy telephone.</li><li>Build with wooden blocks.</li><li>Cook and wash up with toy kitchens.</li><li>Use foam puzzles.</li><li>Sing songs, rhymes and stories.</li><li>Listen to Sesame Street and The Wiggles songs.</li><li>Read Dr. Seuss books.</li><li>Play matching games and card games like fish.</li></ul>

	▪ Play with dolls houses. ▪ Play Which hand is it in? and Which cup is it under? ▪ Match shapes. ▪ Recite and sing nursery rhymes.
Ages 5–7	▪ Play concentration and other card games involving memory. ▪ Play spying games. ▪ Repeat key ideas to build memory. ▪ Help young children learn how to focus and concentrate. ▪ Use visual prompts for memory. ▪ Make and play with play dough. ▪ Listen to music. ▪ Draw from memory. ▪ Learn and make up rhymes. ▪ Make and follow trails. ▪ Collect sports cards. ▪ Do origami. ▪ Practise spelling and counting. ▪ Remember objects on a tray. ▪ Learn another language.
Ages 8–11	▪ Help children organise and make notes; develop a system to use. ▪ Build skills in picking out the main ideas. ▪ Use summary hands. ▪ Teach the journey method. ▪ Teach the peg method. ▪ Learn limericks, rhymes and poems. ▪ Map a trail. ▪ Go to a maze.

	<ul><li>Do crosswords.</li><li>Use Cuisenaire rods.</li><li>Join a choir.</li><li>Create history timelines.</li><li>Use maps to draw links with pieces of wool used to connect places and events and times.</li><li>Most schools provide rubrics for required pieces of work. These outline the criteria used to get high points on the project. Try to get some of these and look at what you can help your child do to improve their outcomes.</li></ul>
Ages 12–18	<ul><li>Really emphasise the need for systems to increase memory.</li><li>Go through the revision methods and memory strategies outlined in this chapter with your child and help him or her to put time aside each week to do them.</li><li>Practise magic and card tricks.</li><li>Use the journey method.</li><li>Recite from memory.</li><li>Learn a part for a play.</li><li>Summarise a few newspaper articles.</li><li>Practise note-making.</li><li>Do painting.</li><li>Learn how to juggle.</li><li>Help them to learn key exam terms as well as the study system outlined in this chapter.</li><li>Continue to use rubrics wherever possible.</li><li>Get past exam questions and use these to create practice sessions.</li><li>Learn to play or sing musical pieces.</li><li>Learn funny scenes from films off by heart.</li></ul>

Chapter 13
Practising to improve

One way of looking at this might be that for 42 years I have been making small regular deposits in this bank of experience: education and training. And on January 15 the balance was sufficient so I could make a very large withdrawal.

Captain Chelsey 'Sully' Sullenberger, pilot of US Airways Flight 1549, who safely landed his plane in the Hudson River after losing power.

It's called practice because it doesn't have to be perfect. Most geniuses spend a lot of time practising their skills before they start approximating great performance. Michelangelo became Michelangelo by working incredibly hard.

Practice predicts success. Almost anyone can improve their performance by practising. Geniuses seem to practise and hone their skills and abilities with a passion.

Parents who enforce practice on their children only end up with resentful people who may turn out to be successful but experience considerable periods of unhappiness. Tennis player Andre Agassi was press ganged into a training regime that made him successful but also vulnerable to drug abuse and burnout. It was only when Andre was able to discover his own passion for the game that he became truly great.

Let's contrast Agassi with one of the greatest cricket players of all time, Donald Bradman. Bradman, seemingly without much guidance from his family, preoccupied himself for hours on end with bouncing a ball against a water tank and hitting it with a stick, a task more difficult than hitting a cricket ball with a bat.

The greatest boxer of the modern era, Muhammad Ali, returned from suspension even greater than he had been previously. Combined with his passion to be recognised for his beliefs, he also followed a punishing training regime for six days a week, with only Sundays off.

Artists, musicians and writers all develop practice routines that resemble concrete rituals. JK Rowling wrote her first *Harry Potter* novel in a café. The philosopher Jean Paul Sartre worked for three hours in the morning and three in the evening. Joan Miro created art from 7 am until noon then went boxing and resumed painting from 3 to 8 pm every day. Henry Miller wrote most of his works in the morning. After having a cup of coffee containing precisely 60 beans, Ludwig van Beethoven composed music from dawn until 3 pm. Today, author Haruki Murakami wakes at 4 am and writes for five or six hours when working on a novel.

These rituals can teeter towards the bizarre. Schiller filled his desk with rotten apples, Proust worked in a cork-lined room and Dr Samuel Johnson surrounded himself with a purring cat, orange peel and tea.

As discussed throughout this book, geniuses develop systems that enable them to practically develop their passions without having to make decisions.

Of course, it is highly unlikely that your child will come up to you one day and ask for a desk filled with rotten apples and a purring cat because it is now time to practise. Nevertheless it is a good idea to consider the types of practice that maximise skills to help your child learn.

This is not about drilling kids into a rigid routine of skill development. It's about helping kids to have fun and gain a sense of success as they acquire mastery in areas they are passionate about.

Use your mirror neurons

In the rear part of our prefrontal cortex are situated some very special brain cells called mirror neurons. These mirror neurons activate when we watch other people doing intentional activities and they help us to understand how we learn from imitation and role modelling.

We learn by watching successful people in action. Some of our most important learning happens when we are doing nothing except watching.

For you, this means finding a way of showing your children the very best performers in areas in which they show interest. You learn just by watching masters at work. Whether it is watching Michael Jordan play basketball, Jane Goodall interacting with mountain gorillas, Stephen Hawking talking about physics, or the world's most avid stamp collector discussing her collection, expose your children to the very best the world has to offer.

When you watch someone who is extremely accomplished at something with your child, there are two main ways to do it. The first one is destructive. In this way you marvel at the person's natural gifts and talents, and convey a sense that they have abilities beyond those of mere mortals. This conveys a sense that their level of skill is beyond the abilities of your child. The other way is constructive. This means marvelling at the performance and then pointing out the dedication and hours of practice that person must have put in to be able to do it.

Deliberate practice

It's not just any old practice routine that brings forth genius.

Deliberate practice is where you identify the areas you need to improve on and target them as areas to practise. Most of us fall into the easy trap of practising the things we are already good at. It feels good. We gain a sense of accomplishment. But if we really want to improve at something we need to find the areas where we are not so competent and focus on developing those areas.

To return to our Albert and Rex analogy for our brain, our Rex wants the easy life and is incredibly distractible. That's why people procrastinate to avoid doing something they perceive as difficult or challenging. It always seems easier to put it off until later. The problem is the right time never arrives.

For you, this means helping your children focus on their strengths and to also identify a few areas they would like to improve in. As the pressure to perform well inhibits some children from trying new things, you may want to label this as experimental practice where they try hard things out without feeling they have to succeed every time.

Try to encourage your children to convert their practice sessions into a challenge to see how much they can improve.

The smaller the target the easier it is to hit

Often, when children set too large a goal for themselves they freeze and give up. Their awareness shifts from what they can do right now to the long-term goal.

When we focus on the outcome too much we get the yips or choke. Our focus moves away from what we can do to what is to be done. In essence we become less present in whatever we are doing. We also become more critical and less observant of what we are doing in the moment.

To avoid this, ask your children to look for small improvements they want to make. Aiming small is likely to result in greater long-term improvements than making a single push towards success.

Repetition

Doing a little bit a lot always beats doing a lot a little bit. Remember, it takes humans 24 repetitions to get to 80 per cent of competence. Repetition also builds mastery and the development of brain connections called synaptogenesis.

One major implication of this is that we improve fastest when we practise something for short periods almost every day, rather than do a practice session once or twice a week.

Spaced repetition pays off even more

Spaced repetition also has a positive impact on learning. Instead of concentrating the study of information in single blocks, learners encounter the same material in briefer sessions spread over a longer period of time.

Spaced repetition produces impressive results. A study completed at the University of California in San Diego in 2007 found that Year 8 history students who relied on a spaced approach to learning had nearly double the retention rate of students who studied the same material in consolidated units.

This research implies that the more times students encounter information the more likely they are to understand and retain it.

Mixing it up and interleaving

Mixing up tasks also pays off. Mixing it up, or interleaving, is when children practise different types of skills and it powerfully increases results. For example, you might ask children to do a short set of subtraction problems, some reading, some writing and then some addition problems.

A study published in the *Journal of applied cognitive psychology* asked 10-year-olds to work on solving four different types of mathematical problems and then take a test evaluating how well they had learned. The scores of those whose practice problems were mixed up were more than double the scores of those students who had practised one kind of problem at a time.

Learning occurs in a context. Spaced repetition of the same problem in a variety of contexts increases outcomes. Spaced repetition of a specific skill in a series of different contexts also pays off. For example, shooting goals from different angles.

Covering the same concept five times within different contexts is better than covering five different concepts.

Brain leaps

Research also suggests that it is when we shift from one area of learning to a dissimilar area that we learn fastest.

For example, if you have a chemistry lesson and then followed this with a physics lesson the skills gained in both lessons would conflict and you would improve more slowly. If instead you mix up the areas of learning more and shift from English to Mathematics to Art and then to Science the skills learned in each would remain distinct and outcomes improve. This also applies to any study schedules your child might develop.

Self-explanations

Practice also helps us to get the sequences of what we need to do into our heads.

Children who are able to explain to themselves the steps involved in solving academic problems achieve better academic results. They learn to mentally go through the steps of solving a problem.

For example, articulating the steps of 'First I've got to do ... then I need to ... and then I can ...' utilises one of the most powerful brain abilities – patterning knowledge. This also applies to learning a new sports skill.

Ask your children to outline the process of solving problems. Remember, explaining a process to others builds reasoning skills and clarifies thinking. Additionally, explaining or reasoning out the process of any problem makes you more present in the moment, and thus more open to improvement.

Resilience-based coaching for parents

Coercion doesn't work, encouragement does. It is not useful for parents to be continually pointing out errors to children. Nor is it useful to have parents gushing over every attempt a child makes.

Instead you can help your children to practise in the areas they want to improve by being a catalyst for analysis. There are several steps in this conversation.

1 Break down a task into segments. It could be different parts of an assignment that is due in a few weeks at school, it could be a musical piece, or a foreign language they are learning.
2 Ask your child to rate their level of confidence in each segment or component. You might ask them to rate themselves out of ten with zero equalling totally incompetent and ten equalling mastery. Children will vary in terms of the accuracy of their rating, but just accept it.
3 Then ask them how many points further up the scale they would like to work on next. Aim for about a two-point jump. So if a child assessed his or her skill at spelling at five out of ten, you might discuss what seven out of ten would look like. Ask them to describe what they see as the difference between their current rating and a few points up the scale.

For example, 'So you say you are a five out of ten speller at the moment, but you'd like to be a seven out of ten speller.' Tell me what you think you would be able to do if you were a seven out of ten speller?'

If children rate themselves at two out of ten but want to be ten out of ten, advise them to slow down and break their improvement practice into smaller bits. For example, 'Okay you want to be ten out of ten. Why don't we aim to get to four out of ten in the next few weeks?'

If children rate themselves at ten out of ten, say, 'Okay, let's talk about what a twelve out of ten might look like.'

4   Once children have outlined the differences between their current performance and two points further up the scale, ask them to notice when that happens. If a child says, 'Well, if I was two points up the scale I would be able to spell big words like hippopotamus and Mississippi.' You can then say, 'So just notice when you spell those words correctly and let me know.'

As Timothy Gallwey discovered, directing people's awareness is much more powerful than giving pep talks or even giving direct instructions about how to improve. (See more about his coaching methods in Chapter 8.)

5   You might like to leave the matter there and resolve to positively comment on your child's efforts to improve, or you could ask your child, 'Would you like to work out a system for practising the hard bits as well as the easy bits?' For example, if they are learning a musical piece they might break the entire performance into a series of segments, rate each one and then spend more time practising the harder parts.

If your children are struggling in mathematics, you might ask them to rate their level of confidence in addition, subtraction, division and multiplication and then plan to spend more time on the ones that they are less competent in.

How practice applies to school success

Almost everyone gets stressed when there are major exams and assessments. Even successful students who perform well on practice questions can find their performance drops in test conditions.

One of the biggest barriers your children face at school is not their level of intelligence. They have enough intellectual power. The biggest barrier is anxiety. The best way to reduce anxiety is to have a practice routine.

Students who spend ten minutes writing about their worries before mathematics tests at school perform roughly 15 per cent better than those who just sit and do nothing before an exam.

Remember that anxiety raises levels of cortisol, which shuts down memory and language processing. Mathematics problems presented horizontally seems to be more reliant on verbal brain processing than the same problems presented vertically.

$$10 - 5 = 5 \qquad \text{versus} \qquad \begin{array}{r} 10 \\ -5 \\ \hline 5 \end{array}$$

If an anxious child is having difficulty understanding the first example $(10 - 5 = 5)$, which is processed by the brain like a sentence and is therefore more affected by anxiety, teach him or her to lay out the problem vertically. Vertically presented problems use more spatial reasoning which is less affected by a spike in cortisal.

The way children interpret feelings of anxiety also influences their performance. Feelings of stress and anxiety often help us get ready for a challenge. If children can interpret their body's response as a call to action rather than an onset of stupidity they will do better.

How you can help anxious children to practise something new

- Reaffirm their self-worth – remind them about their abilities. They know more than they think they do.
- Help them to farewell the fears. Firstly help them to acknowledge what they are worrying about. Explain it and name it. Say something like, 'I'm worrying about this test because I feel it will be hard.'
- Thank the worries for trying to help them get ready to do better.
- Tell children to let go of the worries – don't attach any more brain power to them.
- Move from stress to energy – suggest children use the worry to get some practice done.
- Doodle – if children get stuck, suggest they muck about with things. Their brain is smarter than they know.
- Have children practise under pressure – test using practice questions.
- Outsource their memory – make audio recordings, posters, flash cards or summary hands (see Chapter 11), or use memory methods such as the BASE or journey method (see Chapter 12). Find some way of keeping them organising what they know (see Chapter 11).

Approaching practice in positive ways	
Ages 2–4	■ Have a family policy of the more we practise something the better we get at it, and it is better to try to get something right over many tries than getting it right first time but not really know how to do it. ■ Enrol in Gymboree. ■ Put music on and dance. ■ Start language classes. ■ Learn the alphabet, letter sounds. ■ Read aloud. ■ Draw circles and anti-clockwise circles. ■ Teach letters – start with consonants, eg 'Cat' starts with 'C', 'Snow' starts with 'S'. ■ Read things out loud to them – signs, cereal boxes. Immerse them in natural language practice.
Ages 5–7	■ Tell kids that practice is a time to try things out that might be difficult – no-one expects you to get it right. ■ Utilise mirror neurons – have your children see you trying new things out and practising them. ■ Do gymnastics. ■ Go bike riding. ■ Enrol in ballet classes. ■ Practise swimming and diving. ■ Do tumbling. ■ Play snakes and ladders. ■ Have magnetic letters on the refrigerator and get them to make words and sentences. ■ Learn to count to 100. ■ Practise counting by 2s, 5s, 10s.

Ages 8–11	■ Avoid giving children the impression that learning and practising aren't things adults need to do. ■ Talk to children about the amount of work that accomplished performers in any field put into refining their skills. ■ Encourage children to try the tough shot, spell the hard words, practise something they haven't been successful at – doing the tough stuff and eventually succeeding can be great fun. ■ Turn practice into a challenge game. ■ Go to mini golf. ■ Book in for tenpin bowling. ■ Balance on a beam. ■ Go horseriding. ■ Make masks. ■ Have paper plane competitions. ■ Play ping pong. ■ Do button art. ■ Enrol in drama classes or put on plays at home.
Ages 12–18	■ Teach teenagers the role of repetition and interleaving (mixing it up) in improving practice. ■ Ask them to explain a process to you (so they can learn to explain it to themselves). ■ Start the resilience-based coaching method during their childhood years but really use it a lot when they are teenagers; geniuses start before they are ready. ■ Play tennis. ■ Go surfing. ■ Take them to a skateboarding park. ■ Act out as zombies, vampires or pirates.

CHAPTER 14

Powering up the genius brain

*I bought you a tuna sandwich. They say it's brain food.
I guess its because there's so much dolphin in it, and you
know how smart they are.*

Marge Simpson

To give your children's inner genius the opportunity to flourish, you need to supply them the most optimal conditions you can. One of these conditions is food. Genius brains need the highest octane fuels we can find in order to perform at their best.

Two processes that build genius brains are enrichment and synaptogenesis (the development of connections between brain cells).

The diagram below summarises the activities that promote synaptogenesis, enrichment, or both.

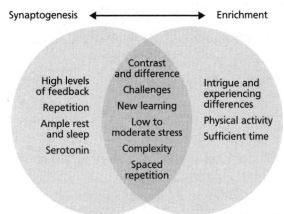

Synaptogenesis ◄──────► Enrichment

High levels of feedback

Repetition

Ample rest and sleep

Serotonin

Contrast and difference

Challenges

New learning

Low to moderate stress

Complexity

Spaced repetition

Intrigue and experiencing differences

Physical activity

Sufficient time

The issues on the left contribute to the growth of synapses and the factors on the right build an enriched environment. We know from many studies that children raised in enriched, stimulating environments develop brains that are far more connected and brighter than those who grow up with no stimulation, play or novelty. The factors in the middle help develop both synaptogenesis and enrichment.

Hopefully the previous chapters have already given you some ideas about ways you can use these genius brain developers with your child. Let's now add a few more things you can do to enrich the environments for your children.

Aromas

Have you ever been somewhere and smelled a particular aroma and found that a whole series of memories came back to you? If so, you know the link between learning and aroma. Memory and aroma are linked. The olfactory nerve develops very early in the human body and links with the hippocampus where memories are integrated.

Aromas such as lemon and peppermint have been associated with increased levels of concentration and relaxation.

Mental alertness	Relaxation
Lemon	Lavender
Cinnamon	Orange
Peppermint	Rose
Basil	Chamomile
Rosemary	

Aromas influence the amygdala. The amygdala is the fight–flight part of the brain. It detects threat and acts quickly to save us. It is also a powerful single trial learning mechanism. For example, you don't need to put your hand on too many hot stovetops in your life before your amygdala warns you not to do that again.

The amygdala also controls emotions such as anger, fear and aggression. Research shows that the amygdala responds powerfully to pleasant aromas.

A balanced, healthy diet

The recommendations made in this section are of a general nature. If you are concerned about the application of these ideas in your child's case please consult a nutritionist or specialised health practitioner.

Eating a balanced healthy diet makes an enormous difference to performance at school and in life. Diet also dramatically influences mood and energy levels.

Encourage kids to drink water

Our brains run on water, glucose and oxygen. Children should drink about six to eight glasses of water each day. Soft drinks never, ever count.

Sugary drinks give you the wrong sort of buzz. Firstly, they make you sick. Just two soft drinks (75 grams of glucose) results in the free radical production of damaged fatty acids called isoprostanes to rise by 34 per cent just 90 minutes after drinking them.

Secondly, they make you stressed. One study at Yale University gave 25 healthy children the same amount of sugar found in one soft drink and found that their adrenaline levels were boosted to more than five times normal levels for up to five hours later.

Diet drinks can be high in caffeine, sorbitol and aspartame and have a negative effect by decreasing concentration and increasing anxiety.

Make sure children eat several smaller meals each day rather than a few big feeds. High protein–lower carbohydrate meals build concentration. Omelettes are better than breads and almost everything is better than french fries. Good proteins include turkey, fish, nuts and yoghurt.

Carbohydrates with a high glycaemic index (refined sugars, refined grains) tell the body to load up with glucose – in the short term they cause feelings of calmness but later on the sugar surges becomes sugar crashes. Teachers often comment on the association between behavioural problems and inattention in school and either the absence of breakfast or the consumption of a very sugary one.

The first part of the day is not the time for donuts, energy drinks, burgers, rolls or sugary food. Later in the day when kids are more physical may be a better time. Breakfasts should include high fibre foods, proteins, yoghurt and milk. High carbohydrate foods with calcium will help keep children calm.

As long as it is medically safe to do so, having a higher protein intake not only enhances learning, it also assists mood.

Our brains are 60 per cent fat and require omega 3 acids found in fish and fish oils to promote optimal brain performance. The old advice that fish and eggs are 'brain foods' is right. Chia seeds are a great option for kids who can't swallow tablets. Put some in yoghurt or in a smoothie.

Foods that assist the release of tyrosine, choline and phenylalanine – the neurotransmitters associated with thinking and memory – include milk, nuts, bananas, seeds, rice and oats.

Neuro-nutrition

You don't need to reach for the medicine cabinet every time you want to feel better. Often making sure you get some exercise, sleep well, drink fresh water and eat well can make an amazing difference to how switched on you and your child feel.

Foods that improve your mood, sleep and calmness

These are foods that have relatively high levels of the amino acid L-tryptophan. L-tryptophan synthesises in your brain into serotonin the most powerful anti-depressant known to humankind. Serotonin, the brain's natural antidepressant, is synthesised in the body from tryptophan, an amino acid found in foods like turkey, eggs, beef and cheese. These are high protein foods. L-tryptophan first converts into a substance called 5 HTP (5-hydroxytryhtophan), which then converts into serotonin. Serotonin stoppers include alcohol, caffeine and artificial sweeteners.

L-tryptophan also makes you sweeter, calmer and helps you to sleep better. The foods that are rich in L-tryptophan include:

- Almonds
- Cottage cheese
- Lean beef
- Milk
- Omega 3 fatty acids
- Pumpkin seeds
- Turkey
- Wholemeal

Foods that improve happiness, concentration and motivation

L-tyrosine is the amino acid that synthesises in your brain to create dopamine. Dopamine is the neuro-chemical related to motivation and concentration. It helps you to feel pumped and raring to go.

The catecholamines or 'cats' – dopamine, norepinephrine and adrenaline – give our brains and bodies zippiness. Too few 'cats' and we experience concentration and motivation problems. L-tyrosine acts as a cat lifter and is found in beef, fish, chicken, eggs, and salmon. Of course, it's trickier for vegetarians: a chicken breast contains 900 milligrams of L-tyrosine. You would have to eat 144 almonds to get the same effect!

Foods that are rich in L-tyrosine include:

- Chicken
- Dairy
- Fish
- Milk
- Oats
- Yoghurt

It don't mean a thing if you ain't got that zing!

Give children an energy boost by providing them with foods that are rich in the amino acid, L-phenaline. This amino acid synthesises into norepinephrine and dopamine. Not only will having more of these neuro-chemicals improve their get up and go, it will also be good for their memory. Foods that are rich in L-phenaline include:

- Chicken
- Butter beans
- Milk
- Peanuts
- Sesame seeds
- Yoghurt

Keep your sunny side up

Foods that decrease irritability and tension are high in L-glutamine. L-glutamine synthesises in the brain into GABA or gamma-aminobutyric acid. Foods that are rich sources of L-glutamine include:

- Avocado
- Eggs
- Granola
- Grape juice
- Peaches
- Peas
- Sunflower seeds

Help your brain to learn

Choline synthesises in the brain into acetylcholine. When you learn something new, your brain forms a new link or circuit between brain cells. These new links use acetylcholine to form and they are then reinforced by dopamine.

Acetylcholine not only helps us to learn it also protects our cells and our memory. Foods that are rich in choline include:

- Almonds
- Beef
- Beef liver
- Cauliflower

- Egg yolk
- Haricot beans
- Tofu

Balance school and part-time jobs

Many students have part-time jobs in secondary school. Students who work more than eleven hours per week experience a serious decline in academic performance, but having some part-time work is associated with improvements in achievement.

Lighting and mood

Boys often like lighting to be lowered or turned off. This is why men like sheds and hardware stores.

Asking children to sit quietly in a subdued atmosphere enhances storage into long-term memory.

For learning, natural or indirect lighting such as a desk lamp is best. Avoid studying under fluorescent lighting. Schools that have classrooms lit with full spectrum rather than fluorescent lights have fewer missed school days. Fluorescent light raises cortisol levels in the blood stream and can suppress the immune system.

Lighting also influences our moods. Seasonal affective disorder or the winter blues is linked to insufficient light. Natural sunlight ranges from 2000 lux (a measure of a unit of light) on a cloudy day to 100,000 lux on a sunny day. If you are mostly indoors you will only get about 100 lux.

A 150–200 watt globe equals 2 500 lux and there is evidence that using a bright light in the day improves mood.

Movement and exercise

There are good reasons for getting outside and going for a walk. If it's cold, buy a coat.

Exercise brings increased oxygenated blood into our brains. Just standing up is estimated to increase blood flow to the brain by 20 per cent. Some studies indicate boys learn best standing up.

Exercise is good for brains. Short bursts of intense aerobic activity (60 seconds) have a positive benefit on students. Exercise also contributes to neuroplasticity.

Music

Music has a powerful influence over emotion, learning and analysis. Some studies have related Mozart's music to increased intelligence levels. Children who listened to Mozart's 'Sonata for Two Pianos in D Major' for ten minutes raised their test scores in abstract and spatial reasoning.

Listening to music may alter brain organisation. Four-year-olds who listened to one hour of classical music each day had EEG results that suggested more brain coherence and more time spent in alpha states (those that create relaxed awareness).

Overall the research of specific types of music (such as the Mozart effect) in enhancing learning outcomes has been overhyped. Play music that you like and that sets a mood in your home.

When children are learning, play music that is either instrumental or has indistinct lyrics. The music of Cirque de Soleil is one example.

Learning to play a musical instrument is also beneficial. For example, playing the piano increases spatial awareness and ability to think ahead. Learning music also increases listening and memory skills.

Try to match children to instruments they are likely to succeed with. For example, clarinet, piano and advanced guitar all require fine motor skills whereas drums, trumpet and cymbals require gross motor skills.

Parents can help children to develop different playlists of songs for different moods – a rev-up, pumped-up one and a calming-down one.

Second languages

Learning another language changes your brain. Children who learn a second language when they are young – between three and seven years of age – perform like native speakers. After the age of eight, performance declines.

Television

The relationship between education attainment and television viewing is complex.

A study of over one million students found the optimal amount of television viewing related to educational attainment varies with age.

- Under the age of two or three: none.
- At nine years of age: two hours a day.

- At thirteen years of age: one-and-a-half hours a day.
- At seventeen years of age: half an hour a day.

Should I have my child accelerated at school?

The evidence is mixed. Certainly the research indicates that advancing a child's grade level increases outcomes academically but there are pros and cons. You could always consider a partial acceleration. If your child is achieving well above average in mathematics, he or she could participate in maths classes with older students. Look for schools that offer the flexibility of catering for advanced students and always trust your own knowledge of your child. You know you child best and are in the best position to determine the circumstances in which they are most likely to thrive.

Socially, however, it is a different story. You might need to ask yourself the following questions:

- Are the academic gains worth the issues I am likely to face when my fourteen-year-old wants to behave like a sixteen-year-old?
- Are there other ways to achieve the same leap in academic achievement?

To consider the answer to those questions you need to not only power up children's genius brains but give them the routines that will set them up for success.

Optimising children's brains	
Ages 2–4	<ul><li>Give lots of feedback to children.</li><li>Encourage play and discovery.</li><li>Read to them.</li><li>Play counting and numbers games.</li><li>Encourage bilingualism.</li></ul>
Ages 5–7	<ul><li>Encourage physical play and exercise.</li><li>Get them on a good breakfast routine and keep them on it.</li><li>Read to them and with them.</li><li>Establish brain-friendly healthy eating routines.</li><li>Provide opportunities to engage in aerobic activity and brain gym coordination activities.</li><li>Learn to play a musical instrument.</li></ul>
Ages 8–11	<ul><li>Make sure to keep up good sleep habits.</li><li>Help them to understand complex issues by giving hands-on practical and real world experiences.</li><li>Encourage theatre sports activities as a way of keeping them involved in reading.</li><li>Keep television and screen time to no more than two hours per day.</li><li>Learn a second language.</li><li>Play a musical instrument.</li><li>Be a member of a choir.</li><li>Exercise regularly.</li></ul>

Ages 12–18	▪ Avoid sugary and highly caffeinated drinks.
	▪ Keep challenging them to challenge themselves.
	▪ Encourage part-time work for older adolescents.
	▪ Keep television and screen time to a minimum.
	▪ Keep active – exercise regularly.
	▪ Have good wind-down and sleep routines.
	▪ Keep electronics out of bedrooms.

CHAPTER 15

Establishing family routines and rituals

We live in a 24/7 world. Switched on, distracted, over-entertained, hyper-connected, revved up and sleep deprived. The idea that there are specific times of the day when people do things best is a foreign concept to most children.

For this reason parents who want to unlock their child's genius need to consider establishing family routines that help their child's brain to fire on all cylinders.

Let's take you through an ideal day.

Just before dawn ...

It is 3 am and hopefully you and your children are sound asleep. Your body temperature is at its lowest. Even as you snooze on, your brain is still 80 per cent activated. It is busy consolidating memories, restocking proteins, repairing cell damage, and strengthening synapses. Soon you will have one of the 200,000 dreams in your life. If you are a woman you have a greater chance that this dream will be a nightmare. REM or dream sleep is important for memory consolidation.

Not getting enough sleep really makes it hard to have a great day. If you sleep less than six hours, it is like having a 0.05 blood alcohol level.

One week of restricted sleep is like 24 hours of consecutive wakefulness. Sleep loss impairs the body's ability to regulate blood sugar, which means you age faster, and it makes you gain weight. If you are sleep deprived you often feel hungrier and crave carbohydrates.

Between 3 am and 4 am is the peak time for night – that's when the most work errors, and car and truck crashes happen, as well as heart failure and gastric ulcer crises.

 ## Up, up and away!

Waking up causes violent increases in heart rate and blood pressure, and a peak in blood levels of cortisol so start the day as gradually as possible. Ensure children rise no later than 7 am.

The first half hour after waking, performance is woeful, so this is not the time to make major decisions. Encourage children to take a warm bath or shower. Then it's a good time for stretching, and exercises involving balance, accuracy and fine motor control. Tai chi is perfect. (Morning favours the archer and the surgeon, late afternoon the swimmer and the runner.)

 ## Breakfast

Breakfast should be high protein and low carbohydrate to kick-start kids' mood and concentration – a protein shake smoothie with berries, or an omelette and a glass of milk. Avoid fruit juices and muffins. Stay well away from energy drinks. Consider a good quality multivitamin for children and at least 1000 mg of fish or krill oil.

At 8 am blood platelets are more abundant and stickier, making it a good time to shave for those kids who need to do so. Testosterone peaks at this time.

For teenagers who drink coffee, they can have up to two a day. Caffeine binds with the receptors for adenosine, a natural chemical important in wakefulness. Replace coffee with green tea during the day.

Temperature increases across the day from a low of 36.1°C in the early hours to an average of 36.8°C for girls and 36.7°C for boys. Alertness often rises with body temperature.

Pack some water or the remaining smoothie, a few handfuls of almonds and a turkey and salad roll to take for lunch. Don't forget the water bottle. Your child's brain needs to be hydrated.

 Early morning

It's time to get focused. Children are easily bothered by distractions in the early morning, much more so than in the afternoon. So lessen the distractions and don't ask them to multi-task at this time.

What happens when we try to do two things at once is that neither gets completed nor learned. Multi-tasking means it takes 50 per cent longer to do things. And can be dangerous: talking on a mobile phone while driving increases the risk of crash by 1.3 times; dialling and texting triples the risk.

Increase the amount of incidental exercise your child has in a day. Tell them to take the stairs. Going down the stairs is like an energetic walk; going up them equivalent to running. Moderate exercise makes kids feel less tired.

Between two-and-a-half to four hours after waking up, your children's attention will peak. This is the time they can really take in the information they need to learn.

Around 11 am is the peak learning time for the day for most teenagers. Younger children often focus best first thing in the morning while teens learn best in the late morning.

Late morning is also the best time to learn new motor skills such as dance, art, tennis or golf.

Lunchtime

Lunch is ideally the major meal of the day. Try to follow the Mediterranean diet – whole grains, fish, turkey, nuts, pulses, olive oil, fruits and vegetables. Encourage children to sit quietly for five minutes after eating and then walk for fifteen minutes.

Try to keep the time kids eat fairly regular as food intake sets internal body clocks.

Just by living we burn between 50 and 70 per cent of the energy we consume – 20 per cent goes to the brain, 10 per cent to the heart and kidneys, 20 per cent to the liver, and up to 10 per cent for digestion.

If possible, a 15–20-minute nap increases performance and learning. Napping also recharges kids' mental batteries. Winston Churchill said a nap gave you two days in one. Thomas Edison, Leonardo da Vinci and President Lyndon Johnson were all great nappers.

 Early afternoon

Lots of children have a down time around 2.30–3.30 in the afternoon when they make more mistakes and learn least well. This is not a great time for taking in new information or talking through relationship issues. If your children do have to take in details at this time either move around while doing it or teach them to make very good notes.

During the afternoon it is good to have snacks for mood and energy lifting. Almonds and apples are especially good. Some children come home from school like a bear with a sore head. Rex is out of control. Feed them at this time; it changes their moods.

Between 3.30 pm and 4.30 pm – just when teenagers are driving home from school – is a time to drive carefully. Single vehicle accidents are common at this time (as they are between 2 am and 4 am).

Blood pressure runs higher in the afternoon but it's not a bad time to go to the dentist. Anaesthesia for dentistry lasts three times as long as the same amount given in the morning.

 ## Late afternoon

This is the best time for physical activity. Bodies are generally at their best later in the day. Exercise at this time may result in 20 per cent more muscle strength than in the morning. The heart works more efficiently, reaction time is at its peak, core body temperature is at its peak. Most sports records are set between 3pm and 8 pm. Liver function is at its best between 5 pm and 6 pm.

 ## Evening

Have some calm time 20 minutes before dinner. Dinner should be lighter than lunch and at least three hours before your child's bedtime. It takes about 50 per cent longer for the stomach to empty dinner than lunch. Sit quietly for 5 minutes after the family has finished eating then walk for 15 minutes.

In the evening, commence the wind-down for the day. Put small children in a warm bath. An hour or so before bed lower the lights – use lamps, give them herbal tea to sip, quietly go through to-do lists for tomorrow. Melatonin starts to increase in the evening.

If children are learning new information have them listen to a tape or podcast of key information for about 20 minutes.

Get your children into bed in enough time for them to get at least nine-and-a-quarter hours of sleep. Don't allow them to watch TV, play computer games or study in bed. Remember the sleep cycle occurs every 90 to 120 minutes. Try to catch it.

Structuring your family's day

Wake up around 7 am.

Have a higher-protein, lower-carbohydrate breakfast. Drink milk (if appropriate).

Drink water throughout the day. Avoid energy drinks.

Younger children learn best early in the school day.

Older children and teenagers learn best at about 11 am.

For lunch, include 'smile on the dial' tryptophan-rich foods like turkey, lean beef and almonds (if safe to do so).

Down time is often between 2.30 and 3.30 pm – a good time for seeing friends and for physical exercise.

Have a healthy afternoon snack like apples and almonds.

In the evening have a family ritual of lowering lighting, lessening screen time and winding down towards sleep time.

CHAPTER 16
Genius in action

*There is no reasoning someone out of a position he has
not reasoned himself into.*

Clive James

When you live life close to the edge there is always a chance from time to time that you might bleed a bit. Many people are content to dim their lights, to dream smaller dreams than they otherwise might and to live under a glass ceiling largely of their own creation.

When you unlock your child's genius, they will stand out. They will think differently to the mainstream, concentrate on their passions in a world distracted by entertainment, and create and link ideas in outlandish ways. Your child will be a creator not just a consumer.

By standing out, they may become the target of other people's envy. Humans are most powerfully derisive and dismissive of the people who threaten their ideas.

For this reason, it is necessary to help your child also develop a strong moral compass. Genius is often humble and patient rather than boastful and rushing. The focus of genius is often on the fun they can have while making a positive contribution to the world.

To do this you need to help your children set their moral compass by the stars rather than the other boats in the harbour. Teach them to aspire to high ideals. To look for the best within themselves as well as others.

Character is who we are and what we do when we think no-one else is looking. It is about integrity, doing what you say you will do, having your actions match your words and doing the right thing even if no-one else sees it.

Children learn what they live. The experiences that we give children in homes and in schools are incredibly important because those experiences shape their brains.

Most of our values are absorbed rather than consciously learned. It is by observing the world around us and also by acting in those ways ourselves that we shape our own moral compass. For parents this means that living a life of kindness and loving compassion, adventurousness and a willingness to explore life and ideas will rub off onto your children.

There is no point having genius if you don't know how to use it to make a positive difference in the world. This chapter covers some of the positive aspects of character your child will need to make a positive contribution in the world. Obviously, desirable characteristics like honesty, integrity and kindness are all part of being a good person and a good genius. In my book *Tricky Teens*, I have written about the essential conversations parents need to have with their children. If you are interested in a more detailed discussion of this issue you may wish to read this book.

Focused

We live in the age of interruption in which continuous, undistracted thought and conversations are a rarity. Parents and teachers can steer children towards focusing for longer and longer periods. Games, artworks, conversations and projects that take time to complete all help build concentration.

In a world that seems designed to want to pacify our Rex by either distracting or entertaining him, this takes ferocity of spirit and a singularity of focus. As Stephen Covey beautifully put it, 'The main thing is to keep the main thing, the main thing.'

Thoughtful

Questioning cherished beliefs can get you into a lot of hot water. And yet, it is through questioning the status quo that geniuses get their impulses to change the world.

Having conversations with your children around the dinner table starting with 'why is it so?' and 'why couldn't it be more like …?' fuels the fires of imaginative thinking. Nourish and nurture curiosity. As parents, be prepared to watch ideas come forward half-baked and not fully thought through. Play with ideas, twist and turn them until they spark and catch the light.

Teach your children not to take all of their ideas out into the world too early. People can disparage and ridicule worthwhile ideas when they are half-born. Instead teach them to discuss these at home and provide a hatchery for new ways of looking at the world.

Parents can also introduce the idea of discussing thought experiments with their children (see http://www.toptenz.net/top-10-most-famous-thought-experiments.php).

In a rushed world of expediencies, thoughtfulness stands out.

Intentional

In a world that demands instant gratification, it's the person who plans that will stand out. The future belongs to those who plan for it and create it.

Showing your children ways to plan, to weigh up alternative ways of achieving an outcome, and to consider consequences of actions is a remarkable skill. Many people don't do this. Instead they act on the first thing that pops into their mind, and if that doesn't work they then act on the next thing that pops into their mind. A world that doesn't plan can waste a lot of energy doing things that don't need to be done.

Planning develops intentionality. Teach children that there is a link between means and ends. Very few good ends or outcomes come from acting in ways that are immoral or abusive.

Intentionality leads to trustworthiness and clarity of action. Geniuses generally don't waste much time. They follow their interests passionately and with singular, intentional focus.

Despite this, most geniuses don't describe what they do as work. Most geniuses talk about the joy they had in pursuing and discovering an idea or concept. It is only later that they might consider what they were doing to be work.

Decisive

Genius does not always follow the well-worn path. It strikes out on its own, finding new ways to move forward and new destinations to arrive at. Inevitably, this level of exploration will bring times of uncertainty. The best way forward will not be clear.

There are times when we need to act like a hunting dog. To stop. Stand still. Ears pricked. Sniffing the breeze and watching for signs and hints.

The modern world has little tolerance for uncertainty. In a world that requires deep thinking to create solutions to complex problems, a tolerance for ambiguity and doubt are critical. Not knowing is more important than pretending you know.

As the author F. Scott Fitzgerald put it, 'The test of a first-rate intelligence is the ability to hold two opposing ideas in mind at the same time and still retain the ability to function.'

After a time of consideration, we need to make our best call. The process of consciously deciding is so rare that we don't drop ideas or actions that have proved to be not useful. Many of us go into an endlessly repeating cycle.

Teach your children how to make the best decision they can at the time and to then give themselves time to see if it works before either continuing on or pausing to make a new decision.

Persistent

As geniuses set out to create new areas of knowledge and skill, setbacks are inevitable. Teaching children to strive to expand their world will help them push at the boundaries of current understandings, limitations and knowledge. Setbacks come with striving and striving builds expertise.

Loss of motivation is most often about anxiety. Helping your children to know that everyone gets anxious but not everyone lets their feelings stop them is important. Geniuses take charge of their own learning; they develop and follow simple systems. You may not have been taught how to do this when you were young but you can teach your children how to do it.

Positive and confident

In a world obsessed with outcomes and rankings, it takes resolute parents to place their energies into commenting on effort rather than results, on the process rather than the product, on awareness rather than outcomes. Tell your children that they are geniuses. Remind them that they are capable of great things and then focus the vast majority of your comments on the efforts they make.

Freeing children from outcomes allows them to explore, refine and implement their own genius in their own way.

The world will change dramatically between now and the time your children are at the peak of their career or powers. As you can't foresee what will be valued in the future, give up being the judge of it now. What you can do for your children is to help them fulfil their potential by believing in themselves and feeling confident to take actions to improve in the areas they are interested in. By commenting positively on their level of energy, effort and interest, you build this.

Imaginative and creative

A sense of humour is common-sense dancing.

Clive James

The world says it values creativity and imagination but it doesn't really. Schools have largely narrowed their focus to the areas they are assessed as effective by – numeracy and literacy. Look around at the adults you know. How many of them actively play? Oh, they might play a sport, or place a bet or watch football but how many of them play at something for its own sake? They might compete but I suspect very few play.

Consider role modelling the importance of this by reintroducing play into your own life. If you need some inspiration, Julia Cameron's *The Artist's Way* and Nick Bantock's *The Trickster's Hat: a mischievous apprenticeship in creativity* are great places to begin.

Having your child see you play, whether it be drawing, reading, dancing, singing, clay modelling, knitting, writing, painting, sculpting, weaving or doodling, sends a powerful message. Play is the source of our imagination and creativity and it is something everyone can do.

Organised

We have more ways than ever of storing information and yet it seems more people than ever feel overwhelmed. Take stock. Implement some of the ideas in this book about storing, sorting and organising information.

Many people seem almost paralysed into inaction by feeling overwhelmed by the rate of change and the amount of information. Geniuses contribute to society by being able to bring clarity and a vision of what's possible to others. Being able to pick out the essence of an idea, store it, organise it and apply it in new ways allows genius to flourish.

Knowledgeable

If you were to do only one thing out of this entire book to unlock your children's genius, it would have to be helping them improve their memory. The relationship between memory, intelligence and genius are intertwined. Improve memory and you create skills your children can utilise for their rest of their lives.

There are many technological aids you can use to increase the power of memory and learning. I have consciously not included many of these in this book, as many of them will be upgraded before you get all the way through it. For that reason I will make regular updates on these tools on my website: www.andrewfuller. com.au and on my Facebook page The Learning Brain.

Courageous

Building on your children's strengths but encouraging them to do some of the tough stuff first may sound like a contradiction, but it's also the pathway to unlocking their genius.

Genius often involves having the courage to venture into areas where we don't feel so competent and capable. Knowing that making mistakes, and learning how to slowly correct them in areas that we first find challenging, is the sometimes slow and methodical way to improve ourselves. Repetition is the basis of mastery.

Help your children to have tryouts, experiments or have-a-go moments when they practise the things they aren't feeling confident in. The key idea for parents when helping to unlock their children's genius is extension and expansion not acceleration.

Social and playful

Of all of these areas, the most important is relationships. For the vast majority of us, there is no more powerful determinant of our level of happiness than the quality of the relationships we create in our lives.

Teach children how to create good relationships and how to fix one up when troubles arise. Help them to follow the golden rule of relationships: treat other people as you would like to be treated.

Help your child to realise that no-one has correct opinions all the time. As geniuses often think and act differently than the mainstream they can be targeted and hurt by people who are threatened by their ideas. Help them to see the fear that often lurks behind bullying and oppression but not to see it as right or acceptable. People deserve to be treated well and that includes your child.

My friend and colleague Neil Hawkes is fond of citing the philosopher Goethe on this point: 'If we treat people as they are we make them worse. If we treat people as they ought to be, we help them become what they are capable of becoming.'

Most insights of genius come about when people are playing with ideas, concept-juggling and shifting the thoughts in their minds.

So to all of you who are prepared to unlock the genius of your child, thank you for taking this journey with me. I hope this book lingers around your house dog-eared and marked, and is picked up and used from time to time.

In helping your child unlock their genius, there are two more things you can do – learn to revere and respect whatever genius you can find in yourself, and play more.

Acknowledgements

Many people gave me ideas as this book unfolded. All books are to some extent a team effort. This book began over a lunch in Sydney with my stunning publishing team Rex Finch, Laura Boon and Samantha Miles.

A few people took time to read earlier versions of this book and I'd like to thank Vicki Fuller for providing inspirational ideas, Vicki Hartley for her incisive thinking, Lorraine Day for helping me see the beauty of mathematics, Dr Georgie Nutton for her wonderful ideas of nourishing the sparks of genius, Brenda Hosking for her clear and thoughtful inspiration, Peter Wicking for reminding me of how essential grandparents truly are, Mark Holland for his wry insights, Dr Karen McGraw for helping me avoid a few clangers and showing me a few more tricks of the trade, Di Beardall for her pragmatic clarity and insight, Anthony Beardall for discussing how schools can be their very best, and Tim Beardall, who introduced me to the ideas of deliberate practice and why it is not wise to peak in high school. You are all gems!

I would also like to acknowledge the inspiration and scholarship of John Hattie and Mel Lovine.

The following people have also provided ideas, comments and inspiration to this book: Bob Bellhouse, Noel Cranswick, Paul Dillon, Mary Duma, Rod Dungan, Lucy Fuller, Sam Fuller, Neil and Jane Hawkes, John Hendry, Paul Wood, Terry Janz, Nell Jones, Ola Krupinska, Ian Larsen, Catie McNamara, Ron McNeilly, Chris Mackey, Cindy Mathers, Carolyn Meir, Michael Nagel, Ramech Manocha, Peter O'Connor, Bob Sharples, Liz and Trevor Sheehan, Michele Silva, Helen Street, David Tyson, Bert Van Halen, Andrew Wicking, Peter Wiltshire and Paul Wood. Geniuses the lot of them!

Author Notes

Page 4 'The effectiveness of schools is not even based on children's ability to impart the skills that predict academic success.' J Hattie (2009), *Visible Learning: A synthesis of over 800 Meta-analyses relating to achievement*, Routledge: New York.

J Hattie (2012), *Visible Learning for Teachers: Maximizing impact on learning*, Routledge: London.

J Hattie and G Yates (2014), *Visible Learning and the science of how we learn*, Routledge: London.

Page 6 'This trend continues and may even be accelerating.' JR Flynn (2012). *How to Improve Your Mind*, Wiley, Blackwell: Malden.

Page 6 'It is estimated that we process five times more information every day than people did in 1986.' Howard Rheingold (2012), *Mind Amplifier: Can our digital tools make us smarter?*, TED Books: TED Conferences, 26 September 2012.

Page 7 'In contrast today's high school graduate will leave knowing about 2 per cent!' P Ellyard (2001), *Ideas for the New Millennium*, Melbourne University Press: Melbourne.

R Kurzweil (2005), *The Singularity is Near: When humans transcend biology*, Viking: New York.

A Toffler and H Toffler (2006), *Revolutionary Wealth*, Knopf: New York.

Page 10 'Studies of divergent thinking … demonstrate that young children are capable of dreaming up new possibilities at genius level but that this ability …' GA Land (1986), *Grow or Die: The unifying principle of transformation*, John Wiley and Sons.

Page 11 'Experiences drive these processes and if we can give children access to these experiences we can help them to become much, much smarter.' N Doidge (2007), *The Brain that Changes Itself*, Scribe: New York.

JN Giedd, J Snell, JC Lange, BJ Rajapakse, BJ Casey, PL Kozuch, AC Vaituzis, YC Vauss, SD Hamburger, D Kaysen and JL Rapoport (1996), 'Quantitative Magnetic Resonance Imaging of Human Brain Development: Ages 4 to 18', *Cerebral Cortex*, 6, pp. 551–560.

K Robinson and L Aronica (2009), *The Element: How finding your passion changes everything*, Penguin: New York.

Page 12 'It took Shakespeare quite some time before he worked out exactly what was wrong in the state of Denmark.' Thomson, C (2010) *What a great idea 2.0: Unlocking Your Creativity in Business and In Life*, Sterling Publishing: Ontario.

Page 13 'Most child prodigies do not grow up to be adult geniuses. They don't even turn into experts.' P Ross (2006), 'The Expert Mind', *Scientific American*, August, pp. 46–53.

EB Burger and M Starbird (2012), *The Five Elements of Effective Thinking*, Princeton University: Princeton.

Page 17 **'Receiving rewards such as stickers when you are learning to read books makes it less likely that a child will enjoy reading for its own sake.'** M Becker, N McElvany and M Kortenbruck (2010), 'Intrinsic and Extrinsic Reading Motivation as Predictors of Reading Literacy: A Longitudinal Study', *Journal of Educational Psychology, 102,* 4, pp. 773–785.

E Schaffner, U Schiefele and H Ulferts (2013), 'Reading Amount as a Mediator of the Effects of Intrinsic and Extrinsic Reading Motivation on Reading Comprehension', *Reading Research Quarterly,* 48 (4) pp. 369–385.

KA Erickson and P Feltovich (2006), *The Cambridge Handbook of Expertise and Expert Performance,* Cambridge University Press: Cambridge.

Page 18 **'I've heard about those new screening tests but I'm not interested in investigating them.'** A similar point is made by Heidi Jacobs (2010) in *Curriculum 21: Essential Education for a Changing World,* ASCD: Alexandria.

Page 25 **'Basically, we have two brains.'** http://oliveremberton.com, accessed 25.11.14.

Page 26 **'It is more fun to call this part of the brain 'Rex'.'** http://www.quora.com/ Procrastination/How-do-I-get-over-my-bad-habit-of-procrastinating, accessed 25.11.14.

Page 29 **'Between seven and eleven years of age, children enter a stage that Jean Piaget called 'concrete operations'.** The Psychology of the Child, (1969) Jean Piaget and Barbel Inhelder, Basic Books. New York. Barel

Page 30 **'Susan Greenfield estimates that over the course of history the size of frontal lobes in humans has increased …'** S Greenfield (1997), *The Human Brain: A guided tour,* Basic Books, New York.

Page 39 **'Geniuses aren't usually all-rounders.'** G Colvin (2008), *Talent is Overrated: What really separates world class performers from everybody else,* Nicholas Brealey Publishing: London.

Page 40 'Usually the stronger team or opponent defeats the weaker opponent, on 71.5 per cent of occasions according to political scientist Ivan Arreguín-Toft.' I Arreguin-Toft, *How the Weak win Wars,* http://web.stanford.edu/class/ polisci211z/2.2/Arreguin-Toft%20IS%202001.pdf, accessed 25.11.14.

M Gladwell (2014), *David and Goliath: Underdogs, misfits and the art of battling giants,* Penguin: London.

Page 49 **'… says that we need to think about how to parent a diverse range of minds.'** M Levine (2002), *A Mind at a Time,* Simon and Schuster: New York.

Page 73 **'Alison Gopnik describes them as the scientist in the crib.'** A Gopnik, A Meltzoff and P Kuhl (1999), *How Babies Think,* Weidenfeld and Nicolson: London.

Page 74 **'People think in patterns.'** D Hofstadter and E Sander (2013), *Surfaces and Essences Analogy and the Fuel and Fire of Thinking,* Basic Books: New York.

Page 75 **'The identification of similarities and differences results in a 45 percentile improvement in academic results.'** RJ Marzano, D Pickering and JE Pollock (2001), *Classroom Instruction that Works*, ASCD: USA.

Page 77 **'Oh, the places you can go!'** adapted from Dr. Suess (1960), *Oh, The Places You'll Go!* Random House: New York.

Page 77 **'A better model is proposed by Susan Wise Bauer, author of *The Well-Trained Mind*, who suggests creating with children timelines for all world events that have occurred in an historical period.'** SW Bauer and J Wise (2000), *The Well-Trained Mind*, W.W. Norton: London.

Page 80 **'The way to get good ideas is to get lots of ideas and throw the bad ones away.'** Linus Pauling, www.brainyquote.com/quotes/authors/l/linus_pauling. htm.

Page 82 **'By thinking about what was not there, Mr Goldman took some wooden folding chairs and attached wheels and a basket to them ...'** en.wikipedia.org/ wiki/Sylvan_Goldman.

Page 83 **'There were 5,126 failures. But I learned from each one ...'** http:// www.businessweek.com/articles/2012-12-18/james-dyson-on-killing-the-contrarotator-his-educative-failure.

Page 84 'I've missed more than 9 000 shots in my career. I've lost almost 300 games.' Michael Jordan, www.brainyquote.com/quotes/quotes/m/michaeljor127660.html.

Page 93 **'Clouseau indignantly says to the desk clerk, 'I thought you said your dog does not bite.'** *The Pink Panther Strikes Again*, 1976.

Page 94 **'Superbly illustrated by Douglas Adams ...'** D Adams, *The Hitchhiker's Guide to the Galaxy* series, 1979–1992, The Random House Publishing Group: New York.

Page 99 **'Walter Mischel offered young children the choice between eating one marshmallow straightaway or two when he returned.'** W Mischel (2014), *The Marshmallow Test: Understanding self-control and how to master it*, Transworld Digital.

Page 99 **'David Fergusson studied over 1200 children from Christchurch, New Zealand, up to their thirtieth birthday ...'** DM Fergusson (AQ: date), 'Christchurch Health and Development Study', http://www.otago.ac.nz/christchurch/research/ healthdevelopment/, http://www.hrc.govt.nz/sites/default/files/HRC31fergusson. pdf, accessed 25.11.14.

Page 104 **'A series of other activities has also been shown to assist children in developing the ability to plan, control their impulses and consider alternatives.'** A Diamond (2013), 'Executive Functions', *Annual Review of Psychology*, 64: pp. 135–68.

Page 116 **'Clyde managed to survive because he learned one really important skill.'** James Clear, jamesclear.com/blog http://jamesclear.com/how-to-focus, accessed 25.11.14.

Page 129 'The strongest single predictor of success is your level of persistence.'
Angela Duckworth, https://sites.sas.upenn.edu/duckworth.
A Gorth (2013), 'Student Test Scores Show that 'Grit' is more important than IQ.'
Business Insider Australia, 29 May 2013.

Page 129 'Computer game designers know a lot about what motivates, engages
and keeps the interest of children.' JP Gee (2003), *What Video Games Have to
Teach Us About Learning and Literacy*, Palgrave: London.

Page 129 'If you want someone to keep doing something, dangle success just in front of
their nose ...' BF Skinner, www.simplypsychology.org/operant-conditioning.html.

Page 131 'The neurochemical dopamine is related to our sense of motivation.'
KC Berridge and TE Robinson (1998), 'What is the Role of Dopamine in Reward:
Hedonic impact, reward learning or incentive salience?' *Brain Res. Brain, Res.
Review*, 28, pp. 309–369.

Page 132 'Let's visit the godfather of modern coaching.' WT Galwey (1973), *The
Inner Game of Tennis*, Pan: Kent.

Page 133 'Motivation has more to do with children overcoming their fears than
anything else.' EL Deci, R Koestner and RM Ryan (1999), 'A Meta-analytic
Review of Experiments Examining the Effects of Extrinsic Rewards on Intrinsic
Motivation', *Psychological Bulletin*, 125, pp. 627–688.

Page 141 'Research by Albert Bandura on self-efficacy.' A Bandura (1997), *Self-
efficacy: The exercise of self-control*, Worth Publishers.

Page 141 '... and Carol Dweck on fixed and growth mindsets.' C Dweck (2006),
Mindset: The new psychology of success, Ballantine Books: New York.

Page 141 'Herbert is a Professor of Educational Psychology who identified that
children have two types of self-efficacy: global and specific.' Marsh, H.W. (1990)
'Influences of Internal and External Frames of Reference on the Formation of Math
and English Self-Concepts,' Journal of Educational Pyschology, 82, 1, 107–116.

Page 148 '107,602,707,791 people to have lived on earth.' http://www.prb.
org/Publications/Articles/2002/HowManyPeopleHaveEverLivedonEarth.
asp,accessed on 1 May 2014.

Page 150 '... an unwillingness to try things that the child feels they may not succeed
at.' C Dweck (2010), 'Mind-sets and Equitable Education', *Principal Leadership*,
pp. 26–29.

Page 154 'Creativity is highly predictive of life success in later life.' MA Runco,
G Millar, S Acar, B Cramond (2010), 'Torrance Tests of Creative Thinking as
Predictors of Personal and Public Achievement: A fifty-year follow-up', *Creativity
Research Journal*, 22, 4, pp. 361–368.

Page 154 'But sadly, research tells us that children are becoming less creative.' KH
Kim (2011), 'The Creativity Crisis: The decrease in creative thinking scores on the
Torrance tests of creative thinking', *Creativity Research Journal*, 23, 4, pp. 285–295.

Page 154 '**Einstein played the violin and sailed in order to feel the forces of nature and to seek out inspiration.**' M Currey (2013), *Daily Rituals: How great minds make time, find inspiration and get to work*, Knopf: New York.

Page 162 '**By adulthood it drops to 2 per cent.**' GA Land (1986), *Grow or Die: The Unifying Principle of Transformation*, John Wiley and Sons:

Page 163 '**Edward de Bono's thinking hats can also help to achieve this.**' E de Bono (1999), *Six Thinking Hats*, Back Bay: New York.

Page 164 '**Together they developed the Smart Car.**' www.hybridcars.com/forums/showthread.php?100666-Who...Smart-Car.

Page 165 '**It was mainly used by balding men to regrow their hair.**' www.medicinenet.com.

Page 165 '**Used it to make snow on ski slopes.**' http://www.nytimes.com/2012/02/19/magazine/who-made-that-artificial-snow.html?_r=0.

Page 175 '**Children who can think through and explain to themselves the steps ...**' DT Willingham (2009), *Why don't students like school?* Jossey-Bass: San Francisco.

RJ Marzano, D Pickering and JE Pollock (2001), *Classroom Instruction that Works*, ASCD: USA.

Page 177 '**Identifying similarities and differences results in a 45 percentile point improvement in school marks.**'

Page 178 '**From 2001 onwards with teachers from around the world, I conducted 'practical intelligence projects' looking for some of the more powerful ways ...**' *The Brain Based Learning e-manual*, www.andrewfuller.com.au.

Page 178 '**The note system outlined ...**' This is an adaptation of a note-making model from Cornell University that incorporates two powerful predictors of academic success – note-taking and identifying similarities and differences. lsc.cornell.edu/LSC_Resources/cornellsystem.pdf. I also am grateful to my friends and colleagues who discussed note-making and repetition on Middleweb. www.middleweb.com.

Page 179 '**The problem is it takes human beings 24 repetitions of anything to get to 80 per cent of competence.**' RJ Marzano, D Pickering and JE Pollock (2001), *Classroom Instruction that Works*, ASCD: USA.

Page 185 '**What you do just before you go to sleep is processed in your dreams and your dreams are when your memories consolidate.**' P Marquet (2001), 'The Role of Sleep in Learning and Memory, *Science*, 294, pp. 1048–1052.

Page 185 '**Having additional glucose just before a test or an assessment task increases memory.**' A Mohanty and R Flint (2001), 'Differential Effects of Glucose on Modulation of Emotional and Non-emotional Spatial Memory Tasks', *Cognitive, Affective and Behavioural Neuroscience*, 1 (1) pp. 90–95.

N Morris and P Sarll (2001), 'Drinking Glucose Improves Listening Span in Students Who Miss Breakfast', *Educational Research*, 43, 2, pp. 201–207.

Page 186 **'Another tip for enhancing memory in people is to stimulate their vagus nerve, a cranial nerve that links our brain stem with our abdomen.'** KB Clark, DK Naritoku, DC Smith, RA Browning and RA Jensen (1999), 'Enhanced Recognition Memory Following Vagus Nerve Stimulation in Human Subjects,' *Nature Neuroscience*, 2, pp. 94–98.

Page 187 **'The same rule applies to learning periods, class time and homework time.'** DA Sousa (2005), *How the Brain Learns*, Corwin: California.

Page 188 **'The more actively children are involved in something the more likely they are to remember it.'** DA Sousa (2005), *How the Brain Learns*, Corwin: California.

Page 189 **'Harry's method was to meet all the people in the audience and get to know their name.'** H Lorayne (1963), *How to Develop a Super Power Memory*, Thorson: London.

Page 199 **'Just reading over notes doesn't work. It is boring and can deceive children into believing they know or understand something when they don't.'** PC Brown, HL Roediger and MA McDaniel (2014), *Make it Stick: The science of successful learning*, Belknap Press: Cambridge.

Page 206 **'Dr Samuel Johnson surrounded himself with a purring cat, orange peel and tea.'** M Currey (2013), *Daily Rituals: How great minds make time, find inspiration and get to work*, Knopf: New York.

Page 207 **'Deliberate practice is where you identify the areas you need to improve ...'** G Colvin (2008), *Talent is Overrated: What really separates world-class performers from everyone else*, Nicholas Brealey: London.

J Loehr and J Schwartz (2005), *The Power of Full Engagement*, Free Press: New York.

Page 209 **'Spaced repetition also has a positive impact on learning.'** PC Brown, HL Roediger and MA McDaniel (2014), *Make it Stick: The science of successful learning*, Belknap Press: Cambridge.

C Duhigg (2012), *The Power of Habit: Why we do what we do and how to change*, Heinemann: London.

Page 209 **'A study completed at the University of California in San Diego in 2007 ...'** *New York Times*, http://well.blogs.nytimes.com/2014/10/06/better-ways-to-learn.

Page 210 **'A study published in the *Journal of Applied Cognitive Psychology* ...'** *New York Times*, http://well.blogs.nytimes.com/2014/10/06/better-ways-to-learn.

Page 212 **'As Timothy Gallwey discovered, directing people's awareness is much ...'** TW Gallwey (2010), *The Inner Game of Tennis: The classic guide to the mental side of peak performance*, Random House: [place].

Page 217 This is a synthesis of research from many sources particularly MS Gazzaniga (2004), *The Cognitive Neurosciences III*, MIT Press: London.

Page 219 'Research shows that the amygdala responds powerfully to pleasant aromas.' S Hamann   (2003), 'Nosing in On the Emotional Brain', *Nature Neuroscience*, 6, 2, pp. 106–108.

Page 219 'Diet drinks can be high in caffeine, sorbitol and aspartame and have a negative effect by decreasing concentration and increasing anxiety.' A Mohanty and R Flint (2001), 'Differential Effects of Glucose on Modulation of Emotional and Non-emotional Spatial Memory Tasks, *Cognitive, Affective and Behavioural Neuroscience*, 1 (1) pp. 90–95.

N Morris and P Sarll (2001), 'Drinking Glucose Improves Listening Span in Students Who Miss Breakfast', *Educational Research*, 43, 2, pp. 201–207.

Page 220 'High carbohydrate foods with calcium will help you keep children calm.' D Amen (2005), *Making a Good Brain Great*, Harmony Books: New York.

J Ross (2002), *The Mood Cure*, Thorsons: London.

Page 223 'Having some part-time work is associated with improvements in achievement.' KJ Quirk, TZ Keith and JT Quirk (2001), 'Employment During High School and Student Achievement: Longitudinal Analysis of National Data', *The Journal of Educational Research*, 95, 1, pp. 4–20.

Page 224 'Fluorescent light raises cortisol levels in the blood stream ...' DB Harmon (1991), 'The Coordinated Classroom', in J Liberman, *Light: Medicine of the Future*, Bear and Co Publishing: Sante Fe.

Page 224 'A 150–200 watt globe equals 2 500 lux and there is evidence that using a bright light in the day improves mood.' W London (1988), 'Brain/Mind Bulletin Collections', *New Sense Bulletin*, 13 April, 7c.

Page 225 'Four-year-olds who listened to one hour of classical music each day ...' TN Malyarenko, GA Kuraev, Yu E Malyarenko, MV Khvatovas, NG Romanova and VI Gurina (1996), 'The Development of Brain Electric Activity in 4-Year-Old Children by Long-Term Stimulation with Music', *Human Physiology*, 22, pp. 76–81.

Page 225 'Clarinet, piano and advanced guitar all require fine motor skills ...' M Levine (2002), *A Mind at a Time*, Simon and Schuster: New York.

Page 226 'A study of over one million students found the optimal amount of television viewing related to educational attainment varies with age.' M Razel (2001), 'The Complex Model of Television Viewing and Educational Achievement', *The Journal of Educational Research*, 94, 6, pp. 371–379.

Page 236 'As Stephen Covey beautifully put it, 'The main thing is to keep the main thing, the main thing.' S Covey (1994), *First Things First*, Simon & Schuster: UK.

Page 240 'If you need some inspiration, Julia Cameron's *The Artist's Way* ...' J Cameron (1992), *The Artist's Way: A spiritual path to higher creativity*, Penguin: New York.

N Bantock (2014), *The Trickster's Hat: A mischievous apprenticeship in creativity*, Perigee: New York.